"What an insightful, helpful book! I love the fresh yet thoroughly biblical approach to family discipleship. The emphasis on discipling your family through time (daily, ongoing practices), moments (unplanned, spontaneous occasions), and milestones (special events) will enable you to see more clearly how to bring the gospel into all of life. I've never read a book on this subject with so many practical suggestions for bringing a Christian influence on your children from their birth to the end of their days (and long after you are in heaven). Begin reading this book and I think you'll find, like I did, that it starts strong and gets better with every chapter."

Donald S. Whitney, Professor of Biblical Spirituality and Associate Dean, The Southern Baptist Theological Seminary; author, *Family Worship; Praying the Bible; and Spiritual Disciplines for the Christian Life*

"If you are a flawed parent who doesn't have it all together, but believes that God desires to use you to shape your kids toward knowing and enjoying Jesus, pick up *Family Discipleship*! It's a profound yet down-to-earth guide to help you form a framework for your home that fits your personality and gifts."

David Robbins, President and CEO, FamilyLife

"Yes! This is the framework families need. Both paradigm shifting and practical, this resource will demystify the idea of family discipleship and challenge you to utilize the opportunities right before you."

Ruth Chou Simons, Founder, GraceLaced Co.; author, *GraceLaced*; Cohost, *Foundations* podcast

"*Family Discipleship* is an outstanding resource for families. Like a life raft in a vast sea of parenting advice, this book offers parents a framework for one of their most important tasks when raising children—teaching them to know and love the Lord. Theologically rich, incredibly practical, and genuinely realistic—this is a book I hope all parents put on their bookshelf."

Laura Wifler, Cofounder, Risen Motherhood; coauthor, *Risen Motherhood: Gospel Hope for Everyday Moments*

"In *Family Discipleship*, Matt Chandler and Adam Griffin make you feel more excited than ever to call yourself a parent, while also casting a gripping vision for why we should take discipling our kids seriously. This book is a clarion call to every Christian parent: family discipleship matters, it is doable, and it's our joy-filled responsibility both to God and to the next generation."

Ryan and Selena Frederick, Founders, Fierce Parenting and Fierce Marriage; authors, *Fierce Marriage*

"*Family Discipleship* is a rare resource—intensely practical without becoming a simplistic, one-size-fits-all 'how-to manual.' Matt Chandler and Adam Griffin have provided a framework that challenges and equips parents to fulfill their divine calling to disciple their children in all seasons of life. This book is realistic in its approach, acknowledging the imperfections we all have as parents, and yet very helpful in guiding parents to develop a strategy that fits their unique families. Parents will be challenged to model a life of faith, develop intentionality around God's word, seize everyday discipleship moments, and celebrate life's milestones. Most importantly, parents will be encouraged that this great task of making disciples of their children is empowered by the work of the Holy Spirit through them."

Afshin Ziafat, Lead Pastor, Providence Church, Frisco, Texas

"This is one of the best books I've read on family discipleship! Chandler and Griffin bring wonderful insight to the challenge and joy of everyday parenting—and refreshing perspective on the immense responsibility of disciple making in our own home."

Noe Garcia, Senior Pastor, North Phoenix Baptist Church, Phoenix, Arizona

"Parents have the greatest opportunity to disciple their children, but many parents haven't experienced discipleship themselves to even begin to know how to do that. In the current 'Pinterest-perfect' era of parenting, stress is high for mom and dad as they try to raise their children in the Lord. *Family Discipleship* takes you just as you are, and will show you the way regardless of your level of confidence. Deep and practical, *Family Discipleship* is highly recommended."

Mark Matlock, coauthor, *Faith for Exiles*

"There is a need and a place for books about how to implement family-equipping ministry in the local church, but that's not what this book provides. *Family Discipleship* fills a very different need that's every bit as important as field guides for churches: it provides parents with the simple and practical tools that they need to disciple their children. Richard Baxter once pointed out to pastors that if they will train parents to disciple their children, these practices of family discipleship 'will not only spare you a great deal of labor, but will much further the success of your labors' as a pastor. This book then provides pastors with a simple way to 'further the success' of their labors."

Timothy Paul Jones, author, *Family Ministry Field Guide*; C. Edwin Gheens Professor of Christian Family Ministry, The Southern Baptist Theological Seminary

Family Discipleship

Family Discipleship

Leading Your Home through Time,
Moments, and Milestones

Matt Chandler and Adam Griffin

Foreword by Jen Wilkin

CROSSWAY®
WHEATON, ILLINOIS

Hardcover ISBN: 978-1-4335-6629-5
ePub ISBN: 978-1-4335-6632-5
PDF ISBN: 978-1-4335-6630-1
Mobipocket ISBN: 978-1-4335-6631-8

Library of Congress Cataloging-in-Publication Data
Names: Chandler, Matt, 1974– author. | Griffin, Adam, author.
Title: Family discipleship : leading your home through time, moments, and milestones / Matt Chandler and Adam Griffin.
Description: Wheaton, Illinois : Crossway, [2020] | Includes bibliographical references and index. | Summary: "Helps parents establish a discipleship plan to raise their children in the love of the Lord"— Provided by publisher.
Identifiers: LCCN 2019059556 (print) | LCCN 2019059557 (ebook) | ISBN 9781433566295 (hardcover) | ISBN 9781433566301 (pdf) | ISBN 9781433566318 (mobi) | ISBN 9781433566325 (epub)
Subjects: LCSH: Parenting—Religious aspects—Christianity. | Child rearing—Religious aspects—Christianity. | Christian education of children. | Discipling (Christianity)
Classification: LCC BV4529 .C4285 2020 (print) | LCC BV4529 (ebook) | DDC 248.8/45—dc23
LC record available at https://lccn.loc.gov/2019059556
LC ebook record available at https://lccn.loc.gov/2019059557

Crossway is a publishing ministry of Good News Publishers.

LB		31	30	29	28	27	26	25	24	23	22	21
14	13	12	11	10	9	8	7	6	5	4	3	2

From Matt:
To Audrey, Reed, and Norah. Thank you for
being a part of this experiment.

From Adam:
To Cassie Bryant and Caroline Smiley, whose contributions
and friendships are essential elements of this resource.
And to the love of my life, Chelsea Lane, and our three boys:
Oscar, Gus, and Theodore. One of my greatest hopes is that
Chelsea and I will get to see generation after generation of
Griffins growing in the knowledge and favor of God.

Contents

Foreword

I remember well the day my pantry was demolished by four elementary-aged Wilkin children on the hunt. For once, they were not on the hunt for food. Their school could earn credits toward the purchase of books and equipment by collecting small pink coupons printed on cereal boxes, can labels, and, as it turned out, just about every item in my pantry. To motivate them, teachers offered extra credit for bringing in a certain number of coupons. The scavenger hunt didn't stop with that first pantry raid. On trips to the grocery store, the kids would choose one cereal over another based on whether it had the telltale pink square printed on the box. The recycle bin and trash can were sifted through. Overnight, we went from unconsciously choosing and disposing of items in our pantry to scanning for a pink square I had never noticed before.

Those pink squares were suddenly everywhere. And by paying attention to them, a lot of good could be accomplished. All we needed was a heightened awareness of the opportunity and an understanding of the goal.

In this book, Matt and Adam want to give you that kind of heightened awareness. They want to bring to your attention three simple opportunities for family discipleship that you already have in your possession but might not have top of mind. Parenting can put us into a fog, rendering many of us in survival mode, ready to pronounce any day in which everyone makes it to bedtime alive as a raging success. But we know in our hearts that more is required of us than survival.

11

We cannot afford to simply make it through the day. Those survival days have a way of turning into weeks, and into months and years. Before we know it, opportunities to point our children toward faith in meaningful ways have fallen to the wayside in favor of just getting by.

But Christian parents want to be those who wisely steward the season of raising children. Psalm 90:12 says, "Teach us to number our days / that we may get a heart of wisdom." We want to be good at numbering these precious days.

My husband, Jeff, and I have raised those four coupon-collecting kids to adulthood. I observe that the common exchange between empty nesters and those whose nests are still full often leans either toward "Just wait" or "Just treasure this season." The first response is not helpful, but to be honest, the second one isn't either. It's encouraging, yes, but it lacks the practicality most young parents are desperately seeking. We do love our children—deeply so—but we want to channel that affection into action. We want to love our children not merely in word or in feeling, but in deed.

You hold in your hands a book that offers not just encouragement, but practical help. Through the framework of time, moments, and milestones, Adam and Matt help you develop eyes to see opportunities for family discipleship that are readily at hand, though easy to overlook. They offer their own experience not as normative, but as a starting point for us to think creatively about how to adopt similar practices to point our families to Christ. I have seen these three tools help the families in my own church and community do just that. It's amazing what we can accomplish with a heightened awareness of the opportunity and an understanding of the goal. I pray this book gives you both.

Jen Wilkin

Acknowledgments

We are inexpressibly indebted to the NextGen and Communications staff of The Village Church, whose input greatly improved the clarity and usefulness of these ideas.

Worthy of particular note from within those staffs are the contributions and advocacy of David Roark. This resource would not have happened without him.

We owe a great debt to Anne Lincoln Hollibaugh. Her ideas contributed significantly to the material, particularly the distinct roles of the family and the church in family discipleship.

We are incredibly grateful for Ryan Jarrell, who patiently and expertly designed our cover. Also, we would be remiss not to deeply thank our editor Tara Davis and the whole team at Crossway who worked untold hours to create a book worth reading and to help readers find it.

While this is an original work, we are far from the first people to write about family discipleship. We formed our own terms and definitions, and went our own directions, but a lot of our thoughts on *time*, *moments*, and *milestones* were inspired by conversations we had about the ideas presented in Timothy Paul Jones's *Family Ministry Field Guide*. Other books like *The Shaping of a Christian Family* by Elisabeth Elliot, *Family Worship* by Donald S. Whitney, *Raising Kingdom Kids* by Tony Evans, *God, Marriage, and Family* by Andreas J. Köstenberger, and *The Legacy Path* by Brian Haynes, as well as the teachings and writings regarding Christian families by Charles Spurgeon and others by Howard Hendricks, also helped us as we formed the thoughts presented herein.

Last but far from least, this resource would not exist without the collaboration and contributions of Caroline Smiley and Cassie Bryant. It started as a meeting in April 2012 simply trying to clarify the discipling role of parents at The Village Church in Dallas. The sweet season when we were all coworkers starting our families and shepherding the families at The Village Church will hopefully pay dividends for generations.

"Let this be recorded for a generation to come,
so that a people yet to be created may praise the LORD."

Psalm 102:18

"Only take care, and keep your soul diligently, lest you forget the things that your eyes have seen, and lest they depart from your heart all the days of your life. Make them known to your children and your children's children." —Deuteronomy 4:9

"We deeply want a revival of domestic religion. . . . The Christian family was the bulwark of godliness in the days of the Puritans, but in these evil times hundreds of families of so-called Christians have no family worship . . . and no wholesome instruction or discipline. . . . How can we hope to see the kingdom of our Lord advance when his own disciples do not teach his gospel to their own sons and daughters?"[1] —Charles Spurgeon

"God has given you one of the greatest privileges imaginable: the privilege of helping shape the future of another human being. Someday your children will no longer live with you—but what will their memories be? Will they only be of bickering or conflict—or will they also be of love and joy and happiness? Don't let your frustrations or weariness crowd out your love."[2] —Billy Graham

"The job has been given to me to do. Therefore it is a gift. Therefore it is a privilege. Therefore it is an offering I may make to God. Therefore it is to be done gladly, if it is done for Him. Therefore it is the route to sanctity. Here, not somewhere else, I may learn God's way. In this job, not in some other, God looks for faithfulness."[3] —Elisabeth Elliot

"God grants offspring and commands that they be brought up to worship and serve him. In all the world this is the noblest and most precious work, because to God there can be nothing dearer than the salvation of souls. . . . There is no greater or nobler authority on earth than that of parents over their children, for this authority is both spiritual and temporal."[4] —Martin Luther

Introduction

Children are immeasurably valuable. You, a parent, are the guardian of an immortal soul, a cherished human being, an incalculable treasure, the very image of God himself. When it comes to parenting, sometimes you get to enjoy it and sometimes you have to endure it. It is wonderful and unpredictable. It is the most fun, upsetting, messy, beautiful, disappointing, and encouraging position in the world. Raising kids is an endlessly challenging adventure, and it comes with a never-ending list of responsibilities. One of the grandest of those responsibilities is the call to all parents to be disciple-makers in their own homes. A disciple-maker is a follower of Christ helping others follow Christ. No matter what your household looks like, your family is the primary instrument and environment for discipleship in all the fantastic and flawed ways that it might be worked out. Your persevering and often thankless spiritual leadership in your home is one of the most important things you will ever do with your life.

Your kids need guidance, and you are their guide. We want to inspire and empower you for the magnificent call on your life to lead your household in befriending and following Jesus, and, as you'll see, that plan does not have to be complicated. If your family already feels overloaded, this plan will not push you over the edge with a new burdensome list of obligations, but rather develop a strategy that helps easily weave in everyday ways for your family to worship God and talk about the gospel of Jesus. The hope of this book is to prepare you to equip your family for the work of ministry and to help them grow up in every way into Christ (Eph. 4:15), following a plan that is well thought-out and sustainable. As you read this book, you will realize that not only can you do this, but you can't *not* do this. To parent without deliberately discipling your child is to build your family's house on a foundation of sand.

God himself has called you to disciple your children: to teach them to obey all that he has commanded and to see Christ formed in them (Matt. 28:20; Gal. 4:19). Whether you are a new parent or your kids are older, our desire is that this resource will get you and your household on the same page concerning how you will address the spiritual upbringing of the next generation. We will help you establish a sustainable rhythm of gospel-centered living through our framework for family discipleship—*time, moments,* and *milestones.* Utilizing the framework will bless your family and focus your discipleship, no matter the number, age, development, or personality of your children.

Inside this book you'll find Scripture to consider, questions to answer, structures to implement, and ideas to try out in family discipleship. Answering the questions and filling out the charts are the indispensable core of this resource, building your unique family plan onto the framework. Even if you skim everything else, don't skip those. Consider answering the questions and filling out the charts with the invited insight of a mentor couple, counselor, or pastor. Share them with your church community for accountability. If you're married, lean on these tools to get your spouse and you aligned on your family discipleship plan.

This is not, however, a "silver bullet" blueprint for building the perfect family. Inevitably, the ideas you experiment with or efforts you put into the discipleship of your home will not always meet your expectations. We can assure you that family discipleship seesaws between disappointing and delighting. When it comes to discipleship, your kids will not always respond the way you want them to. That is okay; no kids do. You are not doing this solely to illicit a desired response, but out of obedience to the call from God on your life as a parent.

Your family is not the only one whose plans completely fall apart, who accidentally "used a bad word" instead of capturing a family discipleship moment, whose family discipleship time ended in an argument, or whose candlelit family holiday tradition ended with wax in the carpet and a burn or two. Plans fall apart and people fall short. Take comfort that even in the Chandler and Griffin homes, which will often serve as examples throughout this book, we are far from perfect. Not only we, but every mom and dad we know, the godliest men and women we know, have some residue of shame to battle and a great need for grace regarding what they wish they would have done and what they regret saying or doing as they have led their families. At the same time, some of their fondest memories and proudest parental moments came in the midst of family discipleship. There is joy to be mined from the work of instructing your children. "A wise son makes a glad father" (Prov. 10:1), and "the fear of the LORD is the beginning of knowledge" (Prov. 1:7).

As a parent, you will sometimes feel inadequate. That might be especially true when it comes to your own understanding of God or his word or your ability and qualifications to teach it. Set your mind on the promises of God and *his* ability instead of feeling discouraged by a preoccupation with your inabilities. You, Mom or Dad, cannot save your child's soul. Your child's salvation "depends not on human will or exertion, but on God, who has mercy" (Rom. 9:16). If your child's salvation depended on the quality of your parenting efforts, it would not only make parenting overwhelming but it would make salvation impossible. Your child will not love God only if you are a good enough parent, or run from God if you are in any way found wanting as a mom or dad. Just as in your own life, it is by grace through faith that your kids will be saved, "this is not your own doing; it is the gift of God, not a result of works, so that no one may boast" (Eph. 2:8–9). What a privilege it is, then, knowing that God could do as he wishes without us, but that he still invites us flawed moms and dads into how he saves and raises a child to know him.

Unfortunately, not every one of our children will know him. Many of us, sadly, will have prodigal children, kids who rebel and run from the Lord. It is one of the most heartbreaking realities for Christian families. If you find yourself the parent of a spiritually wayward son or daughter, remember this: there is no such thing as a "hopeless case" or a "lost cause" when the God of the Bible is involved. Who can he not redeem? Who can he not transform? "The LORD's hand is not shortened, that it cannot save, or his ear dull, that it cannot hear" (Isa. 59:1). Patience, compassion, grace, and prayer are in order. Also, remember that a prodigal child is not the cruel punishment of a malicious God because of some parenting failure of yours. Repent and redouble your efforts over your parental shortcomings? Yes. But it does you no good to torment yourself repeatedly with *would've* and *could've*. All we have to rely on for our children's eternal destiny is the knowledge that God is "merciful and gracious, slow to anger, and abounding in steadfast love and faithfulness" (Ex. 34:6). God delights to redeem a human soul, and heaven rejoices when even one sinner repents.

God the Father and Jesus Christ are not looking at each other anxiously, crossing their fingers, and hoping you will solve the salvation of your child before it's too late. No one gets to steal credit from God for a child's deliverance from sin, and you should not beat yourself up when, in spite of your best efforts, your children rebel and run from God. You have no boast and no hope but the cross of Christ. That's it! Literally, you have nothing to brag about or feel self-pity for. You have only this, what Christ has done freely for you already. And your only hope for a rebelling child is that the Father would draw him or her to himself and hopefully use you in the process.

Fortunately, discipling your kids is not a task God intends for you to carry by yourself. Yes, you've been given the gift of a life to steward, but you are to parent with a holy deference, asking the Holy Spirit to do what you cannot in a life that he loves more than you ever could— empowered by that same Holy Spirit for all that he asks you to do in leading your family. God never asks you to do anything that he does not empower you to do. In our own moments of parenting remorse, we are reminded that our role is to plant seeds of truth, water them, and pray that God will give them life and growth as we trust in his goodness and mercy over all our shortcomings. Family discipleship requires divine reliance: "Unless the LORD builds the house, / those who build it labor in vain" (Ps. 127:1). Relying on a kind, gracious, and loving God gives us plenty of reasons to be optimistic about raising this generation. Unlike God, you are not all-powerful, all-knowing, or all-present. You are not always right, always just, or always good. But your child's heavenly Father is, and he even loves the lost and wandering sheep. You don't know what the future holds, but you know the one who holds the future—trust him.

Despite bumps along the way, many of us will see faith sparked in the lives of our children through intentional discipleship. We will feel and know the presence of the Holy Spirit in our midst as we gather, and we will have the opportunity to celebrate as we witness God reveal himself to a new generation. Never relent in praying to the Lord for his movement in your family. You and your child belong first and foremost to your heavenly Father, who knows you the best and loves you the most.

Some of you are just starting your parenting journey and might be filled with the optimistic bliss of a freshly germinating family tree. Some of you have been doing this for a while, and the thought of family discipleship may fill you with a foreboding skepticism or pessimism. We could all use a dose of reality. Discipling a family is costly and far from easy. Parenting is hard work, and no one does it perfectly. You will mess up countless times, but leading your family to follow Christ can be simpler and more enjoyable than your moments of doubt may make it seem. No one is pretending the job ahead will be effortless, but do not assume that it cannot be fun and life-giving too. Your God is the God of joy and creativity and imagination.

In Christ, we can absolutely do this, undaunted by the hurdles along the way. In Christ, we can absolutely enjoy this and glory in the fruit of our efforts, for true fruit comes from abiding in the true vine, Jesus Christ. "Let us also lay aside every weight, and sin which clings so closely, and let us run with endurance the race that is set before us, looking to Jesus, the founder and perfecter of our faith" (Heb. 12:1–2). God calls us to join him in witnessing his power in the lives of our children and to take a significant role in his work. Hallelujah!

How to Use This Book

This book is designed to be used by parents to create a plan for the spiritual leadership of their home. Read this book actively—making notes, writing in your answers to the questions, and filling out the charts designed to organize your plan. This will serve to develop your own personal philosophy and methodology for the spiritual leadership of your home. After you've finished the book, use the charts as a reference as you parent, and be ready to readjust as your children's needs change and grow. Be careful, however, not to make the plan take precedent over the person. It is not easy to be a kid. Every plan needs to be built with the person in mind at all times. The plans we want you to make are to serve your family, not, as we might sinfully tend toward, to manipulate a family to suit your plans.

Many engaged couples head to a bookstore looking for resources to help in preparation for marriage. Many married couples likewise shop for books to work through, wanting to work out various relationship related issues. There are a seemingly infinite number of books, devotionals, workbooks, and curricula for couples to choose from. When you become a parent, a similar world of resources opens up to you about how to navigate pregnancy and giving birth. You can find countless books about discipline and setting boundaries with kids. There's even a great and growing reserve of resources on talking with your kids about sex and other sensitive topics. Unfortunately, for some reason, it is much harder to find a good book to help you develop a strategy to lead your kids spiritually.

This is surprising, since Scripture makes the spiritual leadership of the home such a huge priority for parents, to bring up children "in the discipline and instruction of the Lord" (Eph. 6:4). Although many catechisms, kids' Bibles, albums, and family devotionals are available, there is a lack of resources that help parents see why and how to use those tools to disciple their families as part of an overarching plan.

We should say up front that this is not a parenting book. At least, not in the traditional sense. This book is not about helping you navigate learning styles, different formative stages, strong wills, birth order, punishments, obedience, and so on. Those books exist, and many of them are very helpful. This book fits into the missing space that exists in intentionally designing spiritual leadership in the Christian home.

Having some level of accountability will be essential to the sustainability of your family's rhythm of family discipleship. This material will best serve you if it is not read by only you. Our hope is that this book could be read as an aid to help you get on the same page with your spouse or community as you consider your plan to disciple your kids. If you are in a Christian marriage, we encourage you and your spouse to read it together and use the discussion questions to help you get in sync with how you will lead your kids in following Christ. If you are a single parent or if you have an unbelieving spouse, we encourage you to use this resource as a motivator to ask some of your trusted church community to go through the framework of *time, moments,* and *milestones* with you as you consider how to disciple your household together. If you have older children, think about having them walk through this resource with you and offer them the opportunity to foster ownership in it alongside you.

If you are about to become or just became a parent for the first time, we hope that this will be a resource for you to establish good rhythms from square one. If you have been parenting for a while and feel like you are lacking in the area of family discipleship, or if you just became a Christian, we hope using this book will help you gently, patiently, and intentionally redirect your family in ways that will help them see all that they have in Christ.

At the time of writing this book, the Chandler home is parenting teenagers and the Griffin household is still making its way through elementary school. The advantage for you is that we are each in different phases of parenting, and that will likely come through when we share what the family discipleship framework looks like for each of us. We hope our examples are helpful, but obviously every family is different, and different developmental stages mean that every family will have to keep evolving its strategy as they go and grow. The framework can be universally applied in infinite ways that accommodate every kind of family at every stage of life, and we'll do our best to help you design your unique plan.

What We Are Not Saying

Before you dive into this book and hear all that we have to say about family discipleship, it is critical that you fully understand what we are *not* saying about leading your family. The following list is essential reading for understanding the rest of the book.

- *We are not asking you to make your kids the most important thing in your life.* Your first love is Jesus. Your personal priority is to love your God. In fact, you cannot love and *lead* your family if you do not first love and *follow* your God. It's easy to make our kids, whom we love so much, our ultimate love. But that is not what is best for you or for them. While we do not want to diminish the value of any human life, we want to be experts at fighting the temptation to put our family first in a way that usurps following our God. Investment in your kid's talents is good, but there's an insidious nature to hearing how special your kid is compared to others. Remember that you are making disciples whose gifts are to serve the Lord, not arranging a family to center on your kids, even if they have exceptional talents.

- *We are not putting responsibility for your child's salvation on you.* First of all, we are not promising that family discipleship as laid out in this book will lead to salvation for your kids. Your child's faith does not rise or fall based on how well you follow the precepts of this book, nor does it depend on your proficiency as a parent. When Christ calls his people to make disciples, he is not saying that you should or even could make or force your children to be followers of Christ. Making disciples is about stacking and gathering the kindling of truths, but only God can spark the fire in this work. So all the more, seek the sovereign, providential, faith-growing God to save your kids and to use you in the process.

- *We are not shaming you.* We hope that as you read this book, a conviction around leading your family with an eternal purpose will take root and grow. But if you begin to hear convincing lies of condemnation or your heart feels defeated and sinking in shame or guilt, stop reading, take a deep breath, and remind yourself that Christ came that you might be free from sin and condemnation. It is great to walk in godly grief that leads to repentance, righteousness, and lessened burdens, but no part of us is casting accusations of poor parenting at you by reminding you of the work God has asked you to join him in. God is not the god of perpetual disappointment, as many parents tend to imagine him. Don't be so hard on yourself. Brother or sister, please hear us: Christ came not to disgrace you but to offer you grace. Lord, deliver us from evil and equip us for this task!

- *We are not unduly comparing you to other families.* While it is fine to learn from other families and we will share some personal stories in this book, we are not asking you to compare yourself in such a way that you will feel either insecure or superior about your role in your kids' lives. You, and only you, are your children's parent. This is not someone else's job; it is yours. God is not looking at you and wishing your kids had been born into a different household or patting you on the back because you're outpacing your neighbor, but he is imploring you to pick up the mantle of responsibility to lead your family in following Christ his Son in all the ways he has gifted you to do so with your unique best.

- *We are not asking you to fake it.* The nature of being a parent is that your kids have often seen you at your worst. This is why Christian parents have to be fluent in repentance language— owning where we've failed, apologizing to our kids, and letting them hear us as we cry out to God for forgiveness. You are not perfect. We know that. But your life as an imperfect example does not excuse you from the responsibility to repentantly press forward in grace-driven effort toward the goal that God has laid before you, to see your kids come to a knowledge and faith in God and learn from every error and hardship along the way.

- *We are not saying you are alone in this.* Not only do you have in your hands what we hope is a helpful resource from some pastors who care about the next generation, but we would call you to press into your local body of believers to do this together with them. Spur them on to love and good works in their families and invite them to do the same in yours. Beyond the church, Christ himself has promised that he is with you. He commands you to disciple your family, but he does not command you to do this without him.

- *We are not saying every parent is qualified to disciple their kids.* For numerous reasons—most notably all forms of abuse, abandonment, or various forms of besetting sins— parents can disqualify themselves from being in a position of authority in a child's life. This is all the more reason why the church needs to be equipped to rally around a family and to evangelize the community. In the modern pandemic of absentee parents, especially fathers, kids who need a family should find the family of God ready to spiritually fit the bill.

- *We are definitely not minimizing how important this is.* While this entire list is true, we would be unloving to then minimize the gravity of the duty laid on us as parents. You are important to your kids. Family discipleship is important to God and to your family. It's part of why God put this child under your care. We can all confess how our priorities have selfishly been disordered by the things in our life. Where does this sit with your other priorities? Many Christian families would say that discipling their kids is important. We are asking you to consider, How important? Is this the lifeblood of your parenting strategy? We are not saying that having other commitments in your family is inherently destructive, but it is evil to, in any way, communicate by action or inaction that anything else trumps your walk toward eternity as a family.

Do Not Be Afraid

The most common command in the Bible is to not be afraid. It is repeated 365 times. We think it bears repeating as we begin this resource together. Parents, do not be afraid. Yes, discipling the next generation is a daunting privilege, but God is with you, and if he is with you, who can be against you? Can anything or anyone wrestle you or your family away from God? We are confident that God can use you to lead your family to him.

Let this sink in and believe it: it is never too soon and it is never too late to start discipling your household. This adventure starts every day anew for every one of us. Every new day brings new mercies. Every new day brings new opportunities. There is not one day where you are on this journey alone. You are accompanied by the God of the universe, who loves your kids more than you do. He is your children's heavenly Father. Another chance, a fresh attempt, a rejuvenated effort starts right now. Lord, have mercy!

"You shall love the LORD your God with all your heart and with all your soul and with all your might. And these words that I command you today shall be on your heart. You shall teach them diligently to your children, and shall talk of them when you sit in your house, and when you walk by the way, and when you lie down, and when you rise." —Deuteronomy 6:5–7

"But once let the family altar be forsaken, and let parents forget the natural duty of ordering their households before the Lord, and you may guard the church as you will, your labor will be vain: you have cast down her hedges—the bear out of the wood shall waste her; you have taken away the tower of the flock, and when the wolf comes he will find the sheep an easy prey. Christian parents . . . with all my heart would I say to you, do not sin against the child by your ill example or by your negligence as to his salvation, but seek the Holy Spirit that to your own offspring you may fully discharge the solemn duties which providence and grace have thrown upon you."[1] —Charles Spurgeon

"The single greatest reason why we are losing our young people today is that the home is no longer the place where faith is transferred. Parents, the primary purpose of the home is the evangelization and discipleship of your children. You cannot outsource this vital component in the rearing of your children."[2] —Tony Evans

"Every Christian family ought to be as it were a little church, consecrated to Christ, and wholly influenced and governed by his rules. And family education and order are some of the chief of the means of grace. . . . If these are duly maintained, all the means of grace will be like to prosper and be successful."[3] —Jonathan Edwards

"A Christian home is more than a house full of Christian people."[4] —Howard Hendricks

1

The Family That Disciples

No one can help or hurt a child like a parent can. Parents are power-ful. "Father" and "mother" are society's most influential roles, which makes being a parent one of the highest honors and most immense responsibilities. If you are blessed enough to have someone who calls you "Mom" or "Dad," be honored. Embrace that title with great trepidation and enthusiasm, speaking what is true, loving, and kind and making the most of the influence afforded to you.

The role you hold, "parent," is one commissioned by God himself. It is no accident that you are your child's mom or dad. Whoever your children are, born to you or brought into your family, God has know-ingly chosen you to train and care for them, to teach them all that he has commanded. If you are a parent, you are automatically in the position of disciple-maker in your child's life. A disciple-maker is not, as some might believe, a role reserved for so-called super-Christians. Making disciples is the job of every follower of Jesus. This is your purpose in your home: making eternal deposits in your children. Your faith is more influential than you think. Your family is the primary instrument and environment for discipleship in the life of your child, and your calling in this life is to give the discipleship of your home your unique best. Your child is not only your progeny; he or she is your

29

protégé. Everything you have learned from and about following Christ is to be passed on to your children to the best of your ability.

What Is Family Discipleship?

Family discipleship is the important and mostly ordinary spiritual leadership of your home. Put simply, family discipleship is leading your home by doing whatever you can whenever you can to help your family become friends and followers of Jesus Christ. Christians not only *ought* to disciple, but they *must* disciple if they are to truly follow Christ. This is the quintessential role of every Christian parent. You cannot be a Christian family if you are not a disciple-making family, because your family can't truly follow Christ if you are not doing what Christ commanded—trying to become more and more like him and leading others to do the same.

Discipleship is both what we heard Jesus command and what we saw Jesus doing. Discipleship is essential to both the message and the method of following Christ. Jesus's method of discipleship was not intended to be unique; it was prototypical. He invited people to follow and live alongside him so they might lead others in like manner. He could have started a formal training school. But instead he built his training around time in his presence as he exercised his trust in the Father, practiced relentless love for all people, and carried out his mission with his disciples. The Great Commission is for you to similarly make disciples of those who do not follow Christ, including those born or brought into your home. To disciple your family as Jesus discipled his twelve, think less of your children as students in your home-university and more as apprentices invited to study and exercise the way of God they see in and hear about from you. When your kids ask questions, think of ways that you might give them an invitation for an answer just like Christ did: "Come and you will see" (John 1:39).

Willfully or not, all parents are perpetually discipling the children around them. Children are watching and listening to you as they form their impressions of the world, of faith, and of what it means to be an adult. As a Christian parent, wield that influence to "bring them up in the discipline and instruction of the Lord" (Eph. 6:4). Good family discipleship is both intentional and consistent with a clear goal to see your kids conformed to the image of Christ.

Because it takes intentionality and consistency, it requires a plan. Christian parents should have a strategy. Every household should regularly be designing, adjusting, and reforming a plan for family discipleship. The family discipleship framework this book proposes, presented at the end of this chapter, is a trellis for that plan to grow on. It takes advantage of the many small and large interactions a family has in order to impart the gospel of Jesus Christ and hopefully see the next generation be "born again to a living hope" (1 Pet. 1:3).

Family discipleship assumes two essential truths that undergird this entire resource. First, parents have the potential to be the most influential person in a child's life. Second, God has clearly commanded that the highest priority of parenting is helping children know, follow, and trust him.

Family Discipleship Is Not . . .

Family discipleship is not free-form spiritual exploration. Family discipleship is indoctrination, teaching the doctrines and worldview of God as laid out in his word without yielding to the contrary opinions of the world or apologizing for the potential offensiveness of that truth. *Indoctrination* has become a bad word in our culture that loves the idea of letting children choose for themselves what *they* think is true. What a disastrous deception! To not tell your kids what is true is the opposite of loving. We are helping the next generation navigate a perilous journey of life through temptations and malicious misinformation. Do not set your children adrift in the desert of this world and cross your fingers that they find the narrow path to the sole oasis.

Family discipleship is not using the word of God in order to get your way. It is not using the threat of God's displeasure in order to get your kids to be quiet or sit still or stop bothering each other. Behavior manipulation is driven by fear, but obedience to God is driven by sincere love and gratitude. A well-behaved child is not the same thing as a discipled child. While the Bible has a lot to say about godly behavior, and obedience is an important aspect of discipleship, behavioral modification is not our main goal. It is far too easy to raise a Pharisee, a child who knows and follows the rules of God but whose heart is far from him. We want our kids to be obedient to God not because they are intimidated by him (or by us) but because they genuinely love obedience and they trust God's love and care for them. Family discipleship pursues sincere heart change in kids, true Christian transformation. Being in a position of authority, it is easy to twist the word of God in order to serve your purposes. It is easy to create a home where it seems like God loves us when we are good and is angry when we are bad. The truth of the gospel is that God always loves us infinitely better than we deserve. We obey because he loves us. He does not love us because and only when we obey. Our kids need to be taught that God loves them beyond their deserving and that obedience breeds joy. Likewise, familial love should also be love without petty conditions. Your kids will not always meet your expectations. It is essential that you love the kids you have and not some version of them you wish you had. We want you to have a family that never doubts just how much you love them because in your relationship your affection and commitment are blatantly obvious.

Family discipleship is not a way to raise popular kids. Raising kids who follow Christ means you are preparing a generation ready to be comfortable being different and even looked down upon by a culture that thinks they know better. While it is certainly not the goal to raise kids to be deliberately irritating to the world, it should absolutely be your hope to have children who will not shy away from what is true just because it does, in fact, irritate someone. What you believe as a Christian is offensive to modern sensibilities. Let this sink in: if God graciously saves your child, many in the culture will be repulsed by your child. At the very least, discipled kids will be considered "weird."

Your son or daughter's faith will not impress the world. Your children will be hated because of who your God is and what he is like (Mark 13:13; John 15:19). We need to raise up a generation who is ready to be distinctly different from their peers, righteously abnormal. In a lot of ways, that's the opposite of our natural inclination in how to raise our children. Raising kids who are ready to be hated means raising kids who unashamedly love God even in the face of loathing and alienation. Regardless if the insults of the world are naive or legitimate, we pray your children will be ready to stand firm in the midst of a world that despises them. You will need to put in substantial effort to nurture kids who are ready for that. You are raising kids who will hopefully pursue generosity over comfort, righteousness over acceptance, and selflessness over self-esteem for Christ's sake.

Family discipleship is not a strategy to become an admired parent. Fight the temptation to lead in order to become an impressive mom or dad and instead impress upon your kids their desperate need for a heavenly Father. Your identity is rooted in being a child of God not a parent of your child. This is not about you finding affirmation in the affection or admiration of others. This is not about building your personal legacy or making junior versions of yourself. Family discipleship shapes children into the image of Christ, not the image of their mom or dad. You are not crafting a child to fit a mold of perfection for human admiration and parental pride. This training in righteousness is not a competition or an avenue for egotistic displays of family superiority. Will you get something out of it? Absolutely. It is incredibly rewarding. But that is not why you do it. We do it for the love of our kids and the love of our God.

Family discipleship is not always the most appealing path. Family discipleship is not the path of least resistance. For kids, authority, training, and regulations seem like adversaries to freedom and pleasure. "For the moment all discipline seems painful rather than pleasant, but later it yields the peaceful fruit of righteousness to those who have been trained by it" (Heb. 12:11). The unpruned vineyard does not yield the best fruit. You don't disciple because it is painless. You disciple because you believe it is best to serve and obey the God who knows what is best and is what is best.

Family Discipleship Is Important

Consider all the planning you put into the physical and intellectual needs of your children. You prepare meals. You make living arrangements. You choose a school. You clothe them. You protect and warn them against the dangers of their world. You establish rules, consequences, and rewards. You could not claim to love your child and send them out unfed, unclothed, or uneducated. You could even be arrested for the neglect of many of these needs. Family discipleship is the charge to realign your priorities, to acknowledge that the spiritual feeding and the spiritual covering of your children needs to be as vital to you and your family as your children's physical feeding and physical covering. "While bodily training is of some value, godliness is of value in every way, as it holds promise for the present life and also for the life to come" (1 Tim. 4:8).

Clothe your children? Yes, of course, every day, but also help them put on the full armor of God so that they may be able to stand against the devil's schemes (Eph. 6:10–18). Feed your kids? Yes, of course, every day, but also give them Jesus, the daily bread of life, so they will not hunger or thirst for eternity (John 6:35). Give them a safe place to live? Yes, of course, every day, but teach them to dwell in the house of the Lord all the days of their lives that they may inquire of God and delight in his beauty (Ps. 27:4). Get them an education? Yes, of course, but teach them to discern good from evil and right from wrong, otherwise they will choose what seems right and it will lead them to death (Isa. 5:20; Prov. 14:12). If your children are successful and they get everything they ever want, what good is it if in the process they forfeit their eternal soul (Mark 8:36)? We want you to have no greater joy in your child's life, nothing that even comes close, than that they are walking in the truth (3 John 4).

It is not only important to your kids that you disciple them; it is also important to us—all of us. What could be more revolutionary in a community than a collection of families raising kids to be friends and followers of Christ together? The Lord working through large-scale family discipleship would revitalize a church and revolutionize an entire society. It is the power of God at work transforming lives and overthrowing the rule of sin in our own homes! It is setting whole households and therefore whole communities on mission to love God, love people, and make disciples that make disciples.

Yes, your family discipleship is valuable for the whole church and your community, and the whole church should be invested in seeing your kids come to know their Savior, but you should also know that training your children to know and follow Christ is a job that first and foremost belongs to you. Though you are far from alone in this mission, God rests the responsibility for their Christian education squarely on your shoulders. We live in a day and age where it is far too easy to put off or pass off the Christian discipleship of our children.

Discipling your child is not primarily your church's job, your child's school's job, or your pastor's job. This job is yours. This job is vital and requires your unique best. You are irreplaceable in it. This job begins again for you today regardless of how long you have been parenting. This book is a plea and a tool for you to embrace God's call on you as a dad or mom to intentionally get in your kid's life around their greatest need, their spiritual development. The Lord who has given you this assignment can equip you for it, and he will not forsake you in it.

Sadly, this critical Christian mission has too often solicited nonchalance and inactivity from mothers and fathers, even those who themselves walk with the Lord. Family discipleship is not a joyless duty for which you should reserve some leftover energy; it is a priority of the highest order and the essential centerpiece of your household's rhythms. Making disciples at home is not "one more thing" to add to your list of parental tasks. It is *the* thing, the primary mission and calling that should undergird every single interaction your family is fortunate enough to have. That may seem like hyperbole, but we are trying our best not to do you the disservice of understating just how significant family discipleship is in a Christian home.

Discipling your family is one of the most crucial, weighty, and enjoyable jobs you will ever undertake. It is simultaneously rewarding and draining, fulfilling and frustrating. It is a fantastic daunting privilege, one that should never be taken lightly. Because it is an assignment directly from God himself, we believe focusing on doing it well is worth earnestly putting in all the time, energy, emotion, and painstaking work it may demand. With all your family has going on, you may think you don't have time for family discipleship. The truth is, with all your family has going on, you can't afford *not* to be dedicated to family discipleship.

You face a formidable challenge: to be part of how God raises up for himself men and women who are "blameless and innocent, children of God" ready to "shine as lights" in a "crooked and twisted generation" (Phil. 2:15). Christian parenting often means knowingly instilling unpopular ideas as we teach our kids to obey all that Jesus commanded. We are raising kids the world may hate, and we want them confident in Christian audacity, ready to swim upstream in a godless culture adrift from holiness. Every step of the way, your kids and you will be tempted to conform to the patterns of this world, so pray God would "lead [you] not into temptation, but deliver [you] from evil" (Matt. 6:13) and transform you by the renewing of your minds (Rom. 12:2).

The good news for us is that in a helplessly broken world full of suffering powerless people *all* children who call on the name of the Lord will be saved. But how will they call on him if they do not believe? And how are they to believe in him of whom they have never heard? And how are they to hear about Jesus unless you tell them? And how are you going to tell them unless you strategically spend time with them? Faith comes from hearing and hearing through the word of Christ. Even if your children are difficult and oppositional and argumentative—like the prophet Isaiah said of the children of Israel—let's hold our hands out to them all day, every day (Rom. 10:13–20).

Most importantly, family discipleship is important because it aligns our hearts with what is true, the reality and supremacy of God. You and your children are both mutually dependent on God. In a world of distractions and lies, as well as a pervasive internal desire for autonomy and control, we need to remember the God who invites us into the joy of relationship with and reliance on him. God both demands and deserves your family's worship. What other motivation or justification do you need for leading your family to follow Christ? "Whatever you do, work heartily. . . . You are serving the Lord Christ" (Col. 3:23–24).

Talking about your parenting can be a sensitive endeavor. Understanding how weighty this task is can lead us into a downward spiral of negative reactions. It is easy to feel afraid of how many ways we will surely mess this up going forward or regret opportunities already past. To feel ashamed of our personal and ancestral dysfunctions and to tremble at the thought of passing the worst of our sinful legacies on to a new generation. To feel insecure about our own insufficiencies and inadequacies. To feel a sense of impending resignation, already inclined to give up when it gets too difficult. All these feelings are common, but they are not rooted in the gospel confidence and blood-bought freedom we get to walk in as those who trust in Christ. In family discipleship, as in all else the Lord calls you to, God's "grace is sufficient for you" (2 Cor. 12:9). Christ has commanded us not to worry, so do not torment yourself with disturbing what-ifs. You can have urgency without anxiety.

Family Discipleship Is Mostly Ordinary

Everything that you do with your family becomes a part of your family rhythm. Your rhythm is what your family will consider ordinary, what you do every day or regularly that feels normal. What are the touch points where your family crosses paths on a regular basis? What are the habits that form the sequences of every week's events? Meals, sports, shows, church, sleep, work, vacations, and so much more make up the pattern of your family's life together. Family discipleship, in order to be rightly ordered and sustainable, should not only be something to "add" to your family's routine; it needs to be woven into all of it. It needs to be ordinary. This is the foundational purpose of what we call the family discipleship framework. Having a plan for family discipleship *time*, *moments*, and *milestones* helps intertwine the discipleship of your children into every ordinary aspect of what your family does together and thus creates a sustainable rhythm.

In the Chandler family, we have gotten to see God do some extraordinary things in our kids' lives. We have witnessed two of our kids becoming believers on the same night while in two different places. We even got to be in the baptism waters with them as they shared how God had revealed himself to them. Those moments are every Christian parent's dream come true.

However, highlights are not the norm for Chandler family discipleship. Our family discipleship has often been marked with difficulty. The vast majority of it can best be described as unremarkable. Much of the time we gather as a family and many of the gospel conversations we have are ordinary and less than memorable. In fact, by and large, our family devotionals have felt like they are not working. I don't ever remember thinking, "Wow. That was really powerful." Yet, after all the everyday forgettable and routine interactions we have had, we now see our kids demonstrate what they picked up from our *time*, *moments*, and *milestones*. And we thought they were barely paying attention!

Family discipleship needs to be part of the ordinary rhythm of your family. It takes resolve and intentionality to leverage the times your family crosses each other's paths, even in the smallest ways. Granted, while much of what we teach in this book involves leveraging the intersections of your family's already existing life, dedicating your family to Christ may require sacrificing other demands on your schedule, especially since reprioritizing family discipleship may involve reevaluating how you are spending your time. More common than replacing commitments in order to accomplish our discipling goals will be repurposing your existing family times, bringing profound purpose into the normal everyday intersections of your family's life to make family discipleship ordinary.

Don't expect every family discipleship interaction to be superlative. It's not that we want to just go through the motions in a dry or lifeless manner; but we expect a lot of normal and unremarkable gospel-centered conversations. Family discipleship will sometimes be like a hearty meal and at other times a light snack. On some more rare occasions, your family discipleship will be like a sweet dessert treat to truly delight in. While dessert is great, it is not your main food staple. In order for family discipleship to be normal, it will be best if it's simple. The simplicity of the framework that organizes the rest of this book is intended to help your strategy for leading your family be free from unnecessary complexities and be clear enough to be sustainable, effective, and memorable.

Spiritually Leading a Family

What does it mean to "lead your family"? This is one of the principal questions guiding the content of this book and one we often get asked as pastors. Put simply, leading your family means going first, initiating what needs to be done. It starts with you. Whatever your family needs, meeting the need begins with your action. In the case of spiritual leadership, that means that you are responsible to initiate and maintain a culture of discipleship in your home. It will not happen without you. You have more influence in your family than you perhaps realize. Using your profound influence to line up your kids behind you and say to them, "Be imitators of me, as I am of Christ" (1 Cor. 11:1) is your spiritual leadership.

To lead is to serve. To be a truly great parent you will have to focus your energy on others, not yourself. Christ embodied and taught this reality. "Whoever would be great among you must be your servant, and whoever would be first among you must be your slave, even as the

Son of Man came not to be served but to serve, and to give his life as a ransom for many" (Matt. 20:26–28). For a husband, leading his wife is synonymous with serving his wife. For a parent, leading the family is synonymous with serving the family. You serve to lead. That means to be a Christian leader, you will have to fight the entitlement and pride that comes so easily with authority. Parents are as much mentors and servants as they are masters. Parenting is often draining and thankless work. You have to literally condescend to be a godly parent. You are not to take your position and "lord it over" those under you. Your role is to identify the needs of those under your care and sacrificially meet them. Determining how your family needs to be served is the same as determining how you will lead them.

Spiritual leadership of your home starts with considering the spiritual needs of your home. The greatest spiritual need of your family is every family member's desperate need for salvation in Jesus Christ, to know and trust him. More important even than teaching your kids to trust in the wisdom of God's instruction is teaching your kids about the salvation available to them in Christ. Of course we don't teach only the gospel, we also teach the law, the way to live. Your children will not naturally know how to live, think, and speak in ways that honor God nor how to discern which influences honor their Lord. They will need your guidance. The greatest way to lead and serve your family is to utilize *time, moments,* and *milestones* to teach your family about the good news of salvation in Christ and what it looks like to obey all that he commands.

Creating a Family Discipleship Culture

Culture is built around values, beliefs, and behaviors. Every family has them whether you have identified them or not. Your family has a unique set of personalities and preferences, expectations and rules, hopes and histories. Your family culture is the atmosphere of your home, and it is shaped by how graciously you respond to sin and failure, how you react to accomplishments and good behavior, and many other factors that contribute to your collective family identity. Every family is different but each individual contributes to your unique family culture shaped by your combined values. Some families value athletic achievement. Some families focus on academic accomplishments. Some regularly gather around the kitchen table for a board game or a family meal while others pass each other like ships in the night. Some homes love peace, quiet, and privacy while others don't feel normal if the house isn't boisterous and busy. Some homes are rife with conflict and some are serene. Designing a family discipleship culture takes having a head of household that purposely sets the tone of the spiritual environment. It is a home that makes family discipleship important and normal. It prioritizes biblical values and incorporates them above and alongside the other values and idiosyncrasies of the family's culture.

Some families may go so far as to craft a list of stated values or a family mission statement. It's a worthy exercise to consider the foundational guiding principles of your household. In the Griffin home, on the wall in the hallway leading from our bedrooms is a framed declaration that "The Griffin family will strive to know God, to make him known, and to honor him in all that we do." If we are considering whether or not to go somewhere or do something, we hold the question up to this mission to determine if our family will invest our valuable time in it. If we don't believe it will honor God, we do not do it. We also have a list of stated values. That same poster states that "we value discipline, obedience, repentance, grace, and fun." This is what we build our family interactions around. If you were to spend a week in our home, I hope you'd see the evidence of those values lived out.

Regardless of whether you have a written and communicated set of values or mission, your family has a culture. Having some clear, shared values creates a safe, shared culture. Be intentional about fostering a culture that values spiritual development. Find ways to make that clear in the way you prioritize your time together and the things you discuss using the family discipleship framework.

What Is the Family Discipleship Framework?

Almost all pictures come in one shape, a rectangle. Whether it's a snapshot of a birthday party or a mountain landscape, chances are the picture has four straight sides and right angles at all four corners. Since pictures come in rectangles, so do picture frames. Each empty rectangular picture frame is suited to contain infinite possibilities within its finite squared limits. The frame can hold whatever portrait of whatever moment frozen in time you are willing to put into it.

The design of the family discipleship framework is similar to a picture frame. It doesn't matter what your family picture looks like, it can be put into this four-piece frame. The framework is likewise universally applicable. The four sides of the framework are simple and yet profound enough to provide structure to your discipleship and give you clarity and support.

But what about single parents? Blended families? Kids with special needs? Spiritually divided homes? Older families? We know every family is completely different. For that matter, every family member is unique. Every individual child and every parent is one-of-a-kind, and each person may be different tomorrow than they are today. But some things about families are universal regardless of the makeup of your home. First, as we've said, no matter what your household looks like, your family is the primary instrument and environment for discipleship. Second, your family context can be served by planning around the family discipleship framework.

As simple as it is, this framework can fulfill its function in any family. It can be a valuable resource even in families where members differ in their views of God. Whether they've professed faith or not, we encourage you to include all adults and children in your family in these *times*, *moments*, and *milestones*, while constantly praying that those who have not been born again one day will be.

The four pieces of the family discipleship framework (defined below) make up the backbone of this book and summarize our strategy for the spiritual leadership of our homes. *Modeling* has to do with your personal spiritual life as a parent. *Time, moments,* and *milestones* are our strategy for imparting your faith to your children by building a new gospel-centered and sustainable family rhythm.

- *Modeling.* Serving as a godly example for your family, living out your genuine walk with God, and demonstrating true repentance where and when you fall short.
- *Family Discipleship Time.* Creating intentional time built into the rhythm of the family's life for the purpose of thinking about, talking about, and living out the gospel.
- *Family Discipleship Moments.* Capturing and leveraging opportunities in the course of everyday life for the purpose of gospel-centered conversations.
- *Family Discipleship Milestones.* Marking and making occasions to celebrate and commemorate significant spiritual milestones of God's work in the life of the family and child.

Beginning with the End in Mind

Think about your family. What images come to mind? Think through each member of your family individually. What is each personality like? What does everyone struggle with? What is everyone good at? Now, when it comes to the spiritual life of you and your children, what do you want your family to look like? What do you want them to do? What do you want them to believe?

As we enter into the meat of this book, let's begin with the end in mind. A child disciple of Jesus Christ is a child who loves God, loves people, and imparts what God has revealed to them to others. You love what you know, so if you want to love something more, then learn more about it. That means that much of family discipleship will involve teaching our kids about God and teaching them about people in our efforts to help them fall in love with their Savior and their neighbor. Think about what that would look like in your own home. If we are going to lead a family dedicated to following Christ, what are we asking God to do? What are we hoping for him to change?

We assume that many of the families that are using this book have kids who do not trust Christ. It is important to remember that discipleship begins before conversion. Is it okay to challenge an unbelieving child to learn about, follow, and obey Christ? Absolutely. That does not mean that in every way we treat nonbelievers as believers. But it does mean that in order to plant seeds of truth in our children's lives we do not hesitate to call them to what is true just because they do not believe it yet. In children, heartfelt behavior will often outpace mature belief and will precede genuine conversion. A child can speak a heartfelt prayer and demonstrate a heartfelt obedience long before he or she actually possesses genuine faith and a committed personal walk with God, a heart fidelity.

So let us give every effort to conduct ourselves as parents in a manner worthy of the gospel of Christ, hoping to see him rescue, redeem, and transform our kids and calling them to follow our example.

"Children, obey your parents in the Lord, for this is right. 'Honor your father and mother' (this is the first commandment with a promise), 'that it may go well with you and that you may live long in the land.' Fathers, do not provoke your children to anger, but bring them up in the discipline and instruction of the Lord." —Ephesians 6:1–4

"Let no Christian parents fall into the delusion that the Sunday school is intended to ease them of their personal duties. The first and most natural condition of things is for Christian parents to train up their own children in the nurture and admonition of the Lord."[1] —Charles Spurgeon

"The group consisting of mother, father and child is the main educational agency of mankind."[2] —Martin Luther King Jr.

"So what is to be noted here is that heads of family must go to the trouble of being instructed in God's Word if they are to do their duty."[3] —John Calvin

"[The Bible] constantly directs our view to children, and children's children; teaching us that all the good which we have is to be transmitted."[4] —J. W. Alexander

"A thorough knowledge of the Bible is worth more than a college education."[5] —Theodore Roosevelt

"Parenting brings incredible, indescribable joys. But because our children matter so much to us, parenting can also bring incredible challenges and devastating heartbreak. For such an important task, we need to have our thoughts and attitudes and our dreams and desires shaped by Scripture." [6] —Nancy Guthrie

2

The Foundation

In Matthew 22, when someone asked Jesus Christ, almighty God incarnate, what is the most important command in the entire Old Testament, he didn't hesitate in his answer. Recalling Deuteronomy 6:5 Jesus replies, "You shall love the Lord your God with all your heart and with all your soul and with all your mind." Jesus called it "the great and first commandment" (Matt. 22:37–38). According to God-in-the-flesh, the long-promised Messiah, this is the preeminent command in the Bible—love God with everything you've got. In Deuteronomy 6:6 Moses says that "these words that I command you today shall be on your heart" and immediately follows it with the mandate to "teach them diligently to your children (6:7)". Scripture reinforces this imperative several times. God has clearly commanded that the highest priority of parenting is helping children know, follow, and trust him.

The foundation of understanding family discipleship must be what God himself has to say about it. What Jesus called the Great Commandment (the supreme love for God in Deuteronomy 6) as well as what we call the Great Commission in Matthew 28:19 (the assignment to make disciples everywhere) both have a profound import for the Christian family. The biblical imperative is for believing parents to teach their household to obey all that Christ has commanded, principally, to love and follow God above anything else.

One generation removed from those who first heard Deuteronomy 6, the people of God demonstrated the danger of not passing on God's truth. In Judges 2:10, we see the generation after Joshua, Moses's successor, described as "another generation after them who did not know the LORD or the work that he had done for Israel." Judges 2 says that they "did what was evil" and "abandoned the LORD, the God of their fathers," and that as a result "the LORD was against them . . . as the LORD had warned" (2:11–12, 15). Those who heard Deuteronomy 6 did not pass on Deuteronomy 6. You, however, get the chance to do what they did not. You get to not only keep God's life-giving commandments but diligently teach them to your children.

Diligence implies dedication. You are not just hoping for your kids to know the Lord; you are dedicated and relentless in doing everything it takes to help them know more about their God. Whatever the cost. No matter what. Your child will not escape your house without knowing the life, joy, and freedom that comes with loving and serving God above all others. This is your biblical mandate as a parent.

While Deuteronomy 6 is one of the primary commands to impart your faith to your children, it is far from the only place this is communicated in the word of God. The Bible gives Christians a robust understanding of family. In this chapter we will show you what the Bible has to say about family as well the important distinction between the role of the family and the church when it comes to discipling the next generation.

God invented the family. Its functions and responsibilities are determined by its Creator. All families can find their history and their mission in the Bible. From the Bible we learn that the first family existed before humanity's fall into sin, quickly ran into depravity and dysfunction, and that, from now until Christ comes back or we go to be with him, every Christian family is called to be the instrument and environment for discipleship of every newly forming generation. However, the Bible also makes it clear that parents are not alone on this journey. The

Christian community around the family—the church—also plays an important role in the spiritual formation of children. Ideally, Christian parents and Christian churches are collaboratively discipling kids to know and love Jesus as their Lord and Savior. Whether it is training, resources, mentors, or programs, churches can provide a great level of support to families. In addition, having partners from within our Christian community who resource and disciple in concert with a mom or dad is a gift.

In Our Homes and Churches

The Chandler home has been immensely blessed by the people of our church, The Village. Of course, my wife and I are the two people primarily responsible for the discipleship of our kids, but the church has had a profound influence on our kids' spiritual development and in many ways has equipped us as parents to fulfill that role.

We have often prayed that God would send other godly men and women into the lives of our kids, and he has graciously answered that prayer time and again. We know there are some things our kids feel more comfortable talking through with someone who is not their mom or dad, and we are blessed to have found an abundance of qualified mentors at The Village Church to come alongside us. Having staff members, volunteer leaders, and friends in our church who contribute to our family's discipleship is an essential aspect of how we are raising our kids.

The church has contributed to our family not only by providing leadership. We have benefited from the thoughtful theological work The Village Church NextGen team has put into designing courses and resources that help facilitate our discipleship. We use The Village Church children's ministry "foundational truths" as the doctrinal groundwork for many of the gospel conversations that happen in our home. We have also often depended on the family devotionals and take-home "talk sheets" The Village Church creates for us to use with our kids in our family discipleship times. What a blessing to have subject matter experts creating the resource we interact with every day as a family.

In the Griffin home we love to invite other adults into our Family Discipleship. The people of our church, Eastside, have had a profound impact on the theological formation of our kids. On Sunday mornings, our kids participate in age-specific classes that share the gospel with them on a level they can comprehend. It means the world to us as parents to have other adults we trust reinforcing the truths we are teaching at home. Eastside values age-specific teaching, but they also reinforce the value of the whole family worshiping together. So, while kids are always welcome in service, once a month we have a Family Worship Weekend, where we focus on the spiritual formation of an entire family and shut down most of our age-specific ministries. It is our kids' favorite weekend of the month.

The Two Key Institutions for Family Discipleship

If you know Christ, it is likely because someone told you about him. Who was that? Was it a family member or another Christian unrelated to you? Whoever it was, thank God for how he used that someone! You are now part of an enduring legacy of faithful saints who have not failed to fulfill their duty of transmitting the things of God to their descendants and to the other children in their community. God established two foundational institutions for telling the next generation about Christ, and they function best when their work is cooperative and coordinated. The Lord has called every immediate family as well as every local church to contribute to the spiritual leadership of the next generation.

- *The Immediate Family:* God calls parents to make their home the primary environment for the discipleship of children.
- *The Family of God:* God calls the local church to equip the saints for the work of ministry, including in their own homes, and to share the load of spiritual leadership for the next generation.

What Is the Parent's Role in Family Discipleship?

In many ways, culture has convinced parents that it is better to outsource the education and training of their children to professionals. We send them to teachers, counselors, tutors, coaches, and churches to learn and develop. Because of this reality, many parents walk in insecurity over their parental influence.

There is nothing wrong with utilizing specialists in specific fields for the sake of your child's growth; parents aren't expected to be an expert on everything in the life of their kids. But when it comes to spiritual matters, God gives the primary responsibility of religious instruction and the training of children to parents, as outlined in Scripture (Deut. 6; Pss. 78; 145; Eph. 6). Christian education begins and should primarily take place in the home.

In God's good design, parents are given the closest proximity and greatest influence in the lives of their children. Parents have the incredible privilege of helping their children discover the world and teaching them to know, love, trust, and obey the one who made them. God commands parents to actively and earnestly shape the character of their children and help form their faith. While God calls one generation to commend his works to the next, which is certainly a community undertaking, there is a particular sense in which mothers and fathers are responsible for the spiritual formation of the children entrusted to them. God calls parents to recount the past faithfulness of God, declare his works, and teach his commands. They have a unique responsibility to testify to his goodness, encourage belief, and model glad-hearted obedience.

As parents model love for God and others, they also diligently teach their children the fear of the Lord and obedience to his commands. This looks like sharing the stories of faith found in God's word and explaining not only what God calls his people to do but also why he calls us to do it. Parents have a unique opportunity to teach their children how to see the world and their experiences through gospel lenses.

They also have the privilege, both through modeling and instruction, to show their children how to engage relationally with the Lord in prayer, worship, and Bible study.

Parents are not only the primary disciplers; this is their primary Christian role. Most families are very busy groups of people, pulled in many different directions. If it seems like you don't have time to engage in family discipleship, the opposite is actually true. You don't have time for overtime at work or any of the myriad family activities and other commitments if you don't have time for this. Spiritual leadership is your priority as a parent.

God says that if a man is not leading his household well, he is disqualified from leading the church (1 Tim. 3:4–5). To not engage in spiritually leading a family well disqualifies someone from other roles in the body of Christ. The rest of the church should take their cue from the expectations of their overseers; if this is not going well, then it is time to set aside other tasks and opportunities until it is.

The Dysfunction of Family

The first family in history was also the first family to dysfunction, to twist what ought to be the safest, most loving relationships someone has into a jumble of injurious conflicts and wounded relationships. Adam and Eve sought autonomy from God in the garden of Eden. Their sin, like many of our modern-day dysfunctions, led to blame and shame. They both attempted to find ways to cover their guilt and to shift the blame for their actions to someone else. Their kids, Cain and Abel, experienced a profound sibling rivalry that led to hatred and murder. Since mankind's fall into sin, family has become a broken version of what God intended.

Sin makes family hard. While marriage and family are God's good gifts and design, as in all things, people find ways to distort even good gifts in ways that bring affliction. Domestic dysfunction is pervasive. Sin brings some version of harmful actions, neglect, selfish passivity, and conflict into every family. In some cases, profound sin can even disqualify a parent from being in a position of authority in a child's life, but in all cases family dysfunctions should be addressed. The wounds from family, the people God intended to love us the best, can have significant and long-lasting effects. But even in light of that, family reconciliation is possible in and through the gracious love of Jesus Christ. A scar remains long after a cut is healed, but it's not always painful, though it remains visible. Sin will derail all of our families to an extent, but God's grace is greater.

It is important to note, also, that conflict is not necessarily sinful. Conflict will play a role in every family. It is not inherently evil to disagree. The Christian family will have to find ways to navigate conflict without descending into sinning against one another.

Christians who recognize sin can react poorly to failings. You, like your kids, might feel the undue pressure of perfection that makes anything less than impeccability demoralizing. If the anxiety of perfectionism has taken root in your family, fight it with the knowledge that your perfection was secured in Christ, who is not surprised or disgusted by your flawed attempts at holiness. Or you, like your kids, might have embraced the fact that perfection is unachievable and therefore you'll tend to surrender to your temptations as if sin were irresistible just because mistakes are inevitable. If resignation to sin has taken root in you or your family, fight it with the knowledge that not only has the war with sin been ultimately won in Christ, but many temporal battles with sin are winnable with the help of God.

One of the most common dysfunctions of family is withholding love, affection, attention, or approval because a child has not met a parental expectation. Know that Jesus doesn't love only a future version of your kids, and you shouldn't either. Don't hold back your love for your children until they have achieved something or met a behavioral standard of yours. We obey God because we love him. We do not obey in order to earn his love. In a like manner, we love our children better than they deserve with a love that does not hinge on how closely they've been able to meet our standards. Love your kids for who they are. Some children excel in athletics, some in academics, some in music. You should affirm your children not only for excelling in what you want them to, but also for the ways that God made them, even if they are different than what you had hoped for. If Jesus loved the unlovable, and he calls you to love your enemy, how do you think that should translate to the way you love your family? Sometimes those closest to us feel like they have to face the highest expectations and the biggest hurdles in order to receive or earn our love. God's love is not based on a measured performance. Let that be both a comfort to you as a parent and a cascading comfort to your kids in the way you lead and love them unconditionally.

What Is the Church's Role in Family Discipleship?

The amount of time your family spends at church together or individually pales in comparison to the concentrated time you spend together away from church. For this reason, among others, church has much less potential to be the most significant influence on a child's life compared to your family. At the same time, church plays a vital role in the call to train and care for the next generation.

In the New Testament, a family is often referred to as a "household." The Greek word frequently used is *oikos*. It does not simply refer to two parents and their children or what we might call a "nuclear family." It is broader than what we typically think of when we say "family." A household could include several generations. It could include aunts, uncles, and cousins. It could even refer to nonblood relatives who lived in close proximity. A household can come in all shapes and sizes. This is an important aspect of family for us to understand when it comes to family discipleship. Though godly child-rearing starts with the responsibility of parents, it is a broader church family and network of relatives who are in close proximity to any child who are all called to help bear the burden of teaching the next generation all that the Lord has done and commanded.

Commending the works of the Lord is a command to God's people generally; the community as a whole is to recount God's power and faithfulness, testify to his character, and teach his ways. Deuteronomy 6 calls all of Israel to know the one true God, love him fully, and diligently raise up future generations to do the same. While parents bear primary responsibility, the church family as a whole is also entrusted with the joyful duty of discipling the next generation.

In our culture, the church generally works both organically and organizationally. Typically, when people think of "church," they think of a place instead of a people. But this should not be so! The church is primarily a people, not an institution or location. The organic nature of the church is simply the relationships we have with fellow believers as we walk together in community. These are the men and women who carry our burdens, share our sorrows and celebrations, pray with us, encourage us, and help us through crises.

In this respect, the role of the church is to help disciple children by coming around parents and caregivers with love, support, accountability, and prayer. Faithful brothers and sisters provide additional voices of truth for children, not to assume parental influence but rather to supplement and strengthen it.

The church family also takes care of the spiritual orphan. They draw in those without believing parents and teach them the ways of God. Many of us first heard the gospel from a camp counselor, teacher, coach, small group leader, or friend who loved us enough to share. Discipling the next generation is a community undertaking. Being a parent and having your own children to raise does not relieve you of the responsibility to help other children and families in your community come to know God as well.

The organizational nature of the church exists to help the organic expressions of the church family flourish. The elders of a local church are charged with faithfully preaching God's word and leading the church toward joyful obedience as they follow Jesus and make disciples together. This includes helping parents obey God's call to disciple their children. Church leadership offers spiritual authority, serving and coming alongside families. They extend encouragement, train parents, and provide supplemental biblical teaching for children and students. This may manifest both in age-specific ministries, in curated or created resources, and in considering the ministry of the family in corporate gatherings.

What the Bible Says about Family

God teaches us about our relationship to him through family. As the Creator of the family, God has a lot to say about it. We know the Bible speaks directly about the responsibility of parents and children, but Scripture also uses the notion of family as a poetic device to teach us about God. His word calls us to imitate him "as beloved children" (Eph. 5:1). He tells us that he will comfort his people as a mother comforts her child (Isa. 66:13). The Bible says that God has compassion "as a father shows compassion to his children" and disciplines his people "as a father the son in whom he delights" (Ps. 103:13; Prov. 3:12). Those who are saved are adopted by God into his family: "In love he predestined us for adoption to himself as sons through Jesus Christ, according to the purpose of his will" (Eph. 1:5). Christians call each other brother and sister, and we call God *Father*: "See what kind of love the Father has given to us, that we should be called children of God; and so we are" (1 John 3:1). Though God could have told us to call him anything, he chose the title Father to communicate his relationship to humanity. Even marriage itself is a profound picture of the gospel that "refers to Christ and the church" (Eph. 5:32). You can see how God feels about family by the way he uses family language to describe his people and his relationship to them. He created marriage and family to be a place and people of comfort, compassion, discipline, and forgiveness.

God teaches the inherent value of children. God loves kids. When others considered children a nuisance, a distraction, or unimportant, Jesus rebuked those people (Mark 10:13–16). The Bible calls children a gift from God (Ps. 127:3–5). Children are not property, though they are often treated as such. Children are people. They do not belong to you like a product or a pet. They are souls entrusted to you as a caretaker, but they ultimately belong to God. When you find yourself parenting from a place of anxiety, you may need to ask yourself if this child is yours or the Lord's. Children are not a less valuable version of humanity nor are they potential people. There is no biblical provision for a moment when a person *becomes* the image of God, where they formerly were not. There is no age at which human dignity begins or ends. The inherent value of personhood is present from the very conception of a unique human being. From the womb, this soul is "from the LORD" (Ps. 127:3), given to you, and he will expect you to steward his or her life well. Like the servants who are given talents and expected to steward them well, you have been given a family to faithfully lead. When the Lord asks you one day for an account of how you led your home, we pray he will say to you, "Well done, good and faithful servant" (Matt. 25:21).

God created, loves, and wants faithful marriages. God gave marriage as a gift to humanity before sin entered the world and, in that first marriage, he commanded that they have children and care for them. Even in the first family, God created clearly defined roles. There was one husband and one wife, a marriage design that was instituted in God's perfect garden before sin even entered the world. Their sons and daughters were to come under the authority of their parents. These roles repeat generation after generation. God loves marriage. He says that "he who finds a wife finds a good thing / and obtains favor from the LORD" (Prov. 18:22). God loves to see that good thing celebrated, guarded, and maintained by the whole Christian community. God's people refrain from sex except within the confines of a loving marriage covenant: "Let marriage be held in honor among all, and let the marriage bed be undefiled" (Heb. 13:4). A husband is called to "love his wife as himself," and a wife is to "see that she respects her husband" (Eph. 5:33). Though there are biblical grounds for divorce, the covenant commitment between wife and husband is not to be entered lightly or exited carelessly: "What therefore God has joined together, let not man separate" (Matt. 19:6). Marriage is the bedrock of God's family design. It is a blessing to a child to have both a godly mother and a godly father. Where one or the other or both are absent, for whatever reason, the church should strive to be mother to the motherless and father to the fatherless.

God commands that children are to be cared for and trained. A child is vulnerable. Vulnerable to lies. Vulnerable to hurts. Vulnerable to neglect. They are vulnerable because in every perceivable way, children are born with an innate insufficiency. They need others to care for them. In myriad ways, this is true of all of us. Scripture makes clear again and again that one of the purposes of the family is to care for the vulnerable and to teach what is known to those who have yet to learn. In Psalm 78:7, the psalmist says that the Lord *commanded* the teaching of children so that the coming generation "should set their hope in God" and "keep his commandments." In 2 John 4, John "rejoiced greatly to find some of [the elect lady's] children walking in the truth" just like God "commanded." It is God's express will for parents to teach their children. The apostle Paul communicates the directive from God to fathers regarding their kids, instructing them to "bring them up in the discipline and instruction of the Lord" (Eph. 6:4). For the Christian, family discipleship is in no way optional; this is a command of God.

God commands that parents are to be honored and obeyed. Parents are commanded to train their children, and children are commanded to honor their parents. In the first of the Ten Commandments that deal with interpersonal human relationships, God commands that kids honor their father and their mother (Ex. 20:12). Paul declares that honor includes obedience: "Children, obey your parents in the Lord, for this is right" (Eph. 6:1). As far as parents are "in the Lord," children are to obey their godly instruction and honor and respect their godly position of authority.

God tells and shows us what to teach children. A righteous, God-fearing person will "delight . . . in the law [*torah*] of the LORD, / and on his law [*torah*] he meditates day and night" (Ps. 1:2). God's torah is both his instruction about the way to live and his story about all he has done to rescue his people. Those who follow God will delight in, study, and obey the law and the gospel of God—the instructions and regulations as well as the redemptive story of God's work to rescue a lawbreaking people. We are tasked to tell "the coming generation the glorious deeds of the LORD, and his might, and the wonders that he has done" (Ps. 78:4), most prominent of which is Christ's redeeming work on the cross and his resurrection. Teaching our kids the gospel means teaching them to trust in what God has done for them, and "to observe all that [Christ has] commanded" (Matt. 28:20). We instruct our children to trust God enough to obey what he's asked of us.

Though this implies a thorough understanding of everything in Scripture, some books and sections are more easily applicable to family discipleship instruction than others. Proverbs, for instance, is built as parental instruction. While the wisdom of Proverbs is broadly applicable, the content is written from the perspective of a mother and father instructing their child. Parents, then, can easily impart this knowledge to their families. Take for example, the fatherly advice in Proverbs 23:15–26:

> My son, if your heart is wise,
>> my heart too will be glad.
> My inmost being will exult
>> when your lips speak what is right.
> Let not your heart envy sinners,
>> but continue in the fear of the LORD all the day.
> Surely there is a future,
>> and your hope will not be cut off.
> Hear, my son, and be wise,
>> and direct your heart in the way.
> Be not among drunkards
>> or among gluttonous eaters of meat,

for the drunkard and the glutton will come to poverty,
  and slumber will clothe them with rags.
Listen to your father who gave you life,
  and do not despise your mother when she is old.
Buy truth, and do not sell it;
  buy wisdom, instruction, and understanding.
The father of the righteous will greatly rejoice;
  he who fathers a wise son will be glad in him.
Let your father and mother be glad;
  let her who bore you rejoice.
My son, give me your heart,
  and let your eyes observe my ways.

Proverbs is rich with parental lessons on work ethic, kindness, honesty, humility, generosity, purity, and so much more.

Proverbs is just one of sixty-six books, each of which is replete with stories of the faithfulness of God and instructions on how to live. Jesus taught that the Bible was about him and that to know the Father you had to know him. Therefore, your family discipleship must be all about Jesus as well. When it comes to answering the question of what to teach children, the answer is simple, God's word. In God's word you will come to know Christ.

God does not take family responsibilities lightly. God loves children and does not tolerate seeing them misled. Jesus said that "it would be better for [you] to have a great millstone fastened around [your] neck and to be drowned in the depth of the sea" than to cause "one of these little ones who believe in me to sin" (Matt. 18:6). We see in the priest Eli that even passive parenting, refusing to intervene when we should, is taken seriously by God. The Lord tells young priest-to-be Samuel that he would "punish [Eli's] house forever, for the iniquity that he knew, because his sons were blaspheming God, and he did not restrain them" (1 Sam. 3:13). The New Testament affirms that if a man cannot manage and lead his own household, then he is automatically disqualified from consideration as a church leader (1 Tim. 3:4–5). When talking about vulnerable family members, Paul wrote to Timothy that "if anyone does not provide for his relatives, and especially for members of his household, he has denied the faith and is worse than an unbeliever" (1 Tim. 5:8). God is serious about families following him and loving one another enough to fulfill their roles of parent and child in ways that honor God.

God gives families the gift of forgiveness. Living in close proximity to other people means being exposed to each other's worst moments and least appealing attributes. A Christian family requires relentless discipline, correction, repentance, and forgiveness. "Pay attention to yourselves! If your brother sins, rebuke him, and if he repents, forgive him, and if he sins against you seven times in the day, and turns to you seven times, saying, 'I repent,' you must forgive him" (Luke 17:3–4). This is a profound truth for marriage and parent/child relationships, that "as the Lord has forgiven you, so you also must forgive" (Col. 3:13). That does not mean that there are not consequences or ramifications for sin, but it does mean that a family will be a factory of forgiveness, not holding grudges and cultivating bitterness, reflecting Christ to one another in the relentless way we repent and forgive. "By this all people will know that you are [Jesus's] disciples, if you have love for one another" (John 13:35).

"Be imitators of me, as I am of Christ." —1 Corinthians 11:1

"Train up a child in the way he should go—but be sure you go that way yourself."[1] —Charles Spurgeon

"The process of shaping the child, shapes also the mother herself. Reverence for her sacred burden calls her to all that is pure and good, that she may teach primarily by her own humble, daily example."[2] —Elisabeth Elliot

"A father is a looking-glass, which the child often dresses himself by; let the glass be clear and not spotted."[3] —Thomas Watson

"The teaching which issues only from the lips is not at all likely to sink any deeper than the ears. Children are particularly quick to detect inconsistencies and to despise hypocrisy."[4] —Arthur W. Pink

"I believe that children are, by nature, very forgiving. I don't think children expect their parents to be perfect. I think they demand that their parents be real."[5] —Beth Moore

"One of the most beautiful things a parent can say to a child is, 'Son, I may make a mistake, but I want you to know I'm going to do the best that I possibly know how. And if I blow it, you'll be the first to know.' This is the sign of an honest parent. And an honest parent develops an honest child."[6] —Howard Hendricks

"Knowing what's right doesn't mean much unless you do what's right."[7] —Theodore Roosevelt

3

Modeling

Family Discipleship Modeling: Serving as a godly example for your family, living out your genuine walk with God, and demonstrating true repentance where and when you fall short.

Observing your daily, ordinary example of life with God following Christ will have one of the most significant spiritually formative impacts on your child. Some of your best lessons as a parent are going to be habitually gleaned by your kids as opposed to explicitly explained. What you think, say, and do—your attitudes and actions—as a Christian man or woman make a profound impression on what your sons and daughters will think, say, and do as they grow into maturity. Your conduct is a visual aid for your family's gospel literacy. Your life well lived, walking as Jesus walked, can be more influential than a hundred lectures about your beliefs.

Of course, in order to model following Christ you must *be* following Christ. A hypocritical or duplicitous life will undermine every piece of wisdom you might want to offer before the first word even comes out of your mouth. It is hard to teach someone to swim while you're drowning. As it pertains to family discipleship, for you to lead in the development of spiritual growth for your family, you must personally be spiritually growing yourself. Before you can diligently teach God's commands to your children you must have them "on your heart" (Deut. 6:6–7). No one is asking you to fake a spiritual life for your kids' sake. The personal call you have been given and what would be beneficial for your children to witness is to "train yourself for godliness" (1 Tim. 4:7). We want you to read this chapter considering how you will plan out your own spiritual disciplines as an individual (and if you're married, as a couple) and lead your home by example. Of course, this will include how you can sincerely repent and course correct as you become aware of your failings.

This chapter is about being someone worth imitating in proximity to your children. That does not, however, mean being someone perfect. Illustrating how to address your own unrealized hopes and your unwanted shortcomings is a critical aspect of Christian modeling. Be someone whose model of humility and repentance characterizes how imperfect people should act, think, and speak at all times, and especially when they fail.

When it comes to failures related to sin, repentance—confessing sin, seeking forgiveness, and committing to battle repeating them—is an essential aspect of modeling. Repentance is actually a great place to start when it comes to family discipleship. Sit down with your family to confess how your family leadership or personal example is different than what you truly want, but do not wallow in regret. Ask for grace over your past, and commit to pursuing a godlier version of this calling going forward with accountability and a plan.

Of course, you will have to accept that not everything your kids learn from watching you will be admirable. Unfortunately, some of your least favorite aspects of yourself may turn out to be your most contagious attributes. You'll likely see some of your flaws in full inherited display in your children. Your blind spots and weaknesses can become theirs so easily. That is the reality of being a family. Some of the most natural and deeply rooted lessons happen through unwitting observation and reflex imitation. Therefore, let's work all the more to show them a life worth imitating.

Caring for your own soul is the first step. Your spiritual health is imperative to the health of your family. You cannot authentically lead a family discipleship time or capture a moment if you are not making the time to be with God and thinking of him throughout the day. When it comes to personal spiritual growth, knowing where to start can be a struggle. Some of us have never seen a healthy version of it lived out. It's easy to feel distracted—not to mention the issues we face of timing, scheduling, and consistency. Even when we've set the time aside, spending time in prayer and reading Scripture can seem dry and lifeless. Remember that you are called to be diligent in the care of your own soul, to work hard and not give up easily (Deut. 4:9).

If I asked your children to describe you, what words would they use? If I asked them what is most important to their parents, what would be on their list? What would they say if I asked them how they want to be like Mom/Dad when they are an adult? Your kids learn from watching you, and they are watching even when you don't want them to. What are your kids going to learn from being around you?

In Our Homes

In the Chandler home, I am usually the first one awake six days a week, and one of the first things I do is make a good cup of coffee and spend time alone with the Lord. Which means, by and large, my kids have childhood memories of coming downstairs in the morning and seeing Daddy sitting at the kitchen island drinking coffee, reading his Bible, and writing in his journal. Of course, I'm not reading my Bible just so they'll see it. I do it primarily so I remember that I am a child of the heavenly Father, and that sincerity is part of what I hope my kids pick up on.

In addition to personal devotions, our home has modeled hospitality for our children too. Guests from all walks of life often join us for a meal. Our children have seen us be inviting, welcoming, and hospitable in ways we hope they will carry on long after we are gone.

But for all the great things we could point to that we've modeled for our kids as part of our walk with God there are, of course, many examples of how my life has served as an example I hope they *don't* follow. I am highly critical. In its most useful application, this means that I am really good at helping make things better. However, the dark edge to that means that I catch myself making snarky jabs at things, sometimes when my kids can overhear. It is terrible when you start to see your kids, especially at a young age, criticize things just like their daddy. I hate to think that they might learn from me, "It's okay to harshly tear things down." I have confessed this to them. I have tried to beautifully build something else in its place. I've shared that in a redeemed version of that tendency, our ability to see what's wrong has been given to us by God so we can make things right. That is, of course, assuming that the thing is wrong in the first place. Sometimes we simply need to die to our personal preferences. I've had the opportunity to model repentance. My children get to see firsthand that their dad is still being sanctified.

In the Griffin home, we try to be intentional about inviting our kids into how we love our neighbors. If the Lord gives us an opportunity to minister and it's not prohibitive to have my boys with me, I always prefer to have them by my side. Whether it is bringing a meal to someone, bringing a gift to another family in need, or having dinner in someone else's home as we share stories, we like to have our kids around our neighborhood ministry. We live in a diverse neighborhood. Many of our neighbors are refugees who have escaped something awful in other parts of the world. Through the ministry God has given us here, God has given our sons friends from many different nations, ethnicities, and backgrounds. What began in bringing our sons along as we met and fed kids waiting for the bus in front of our home has blossomed into friendships with people from Rwanda, Sudan, Afghanistan, Syria, Nigeria, Eritrea, and Tanzania. By seeing our heart to serve our neighbors, our kids are catching both a heart for all people and a comfort with being different.

Unfortunately, those we love the most and live closest to often get the least charity and grace from us. I have a shorter patience with my kids than just about anyone else I've ever met. As much as I don't want it, I have modeled annoyance for them in ways that I unfortunately can never take back. It's hard not to believe that when I see them agitated by each other and then respond with irritation instead of kindness that it's not a reflection of how they've seen me respond in my own impatience and selfishness. Lord, have mercy! As much as I want to be a dad worth emulating, there are innumerable ways that I hope these apples fall as far as possible from this tree.

The Two Key Components of Modeling

Two key components are essential for family discipleship through Christian modeling. A godly role model needs to be reliable and relatable.

- *Be Reliable:* Have repentant integrity.
- *Be Relatable:* Have relational proximity.

Modeling Requires You to Be Reliable

In order to model godliness you must be reliable. You are called to be trustworthy, righteous, and repentant. In other words, you are to be a person of integrity. It is joy to the believer to obey the commands and instructions of God as laid out in his word and demonstrated in Christ's life. That is why we operate according to God's moral guidelines, mission, and commands. Reliable parents are honest about their strengths and weaknesses. They are role models of holiness and sincerity in motivation, thought, and action.

If there is something that you would like to see formed in your children, pray that it would be formed in you to model for them. Be a reliable source of living knowledge concerning godliness. For example, if you want your kids to speak kindly, then seek to be the epitome of kindness. If you would like to see your kids grow in patience, then make every effort to be "quick to hear, slow to speak, slow to anger" (James 1:19). All parents want to see their kids grow in self-control. Self-control is the emancipating fruit of the Spirit. It's the strength and resolve to swim upstream against the current of temptation. In a moment of temptation, you want your child to be able to recognize and resist sin. If you want self-control for your family, find ways to share with your children how you personally are growing in self-control.

The standard for your integrity, where you find your moral guide, must be the word of God. If it is not, you are likely to excuse or minimize failings that you should be battling. Reliable parents follow God even when they don't want to, believing that obedience is for their good and their joy. If left to your own moral devices, you will deem yourself innocent in situations where, according to God's word, you need conviction. You know all of your explanations and justifications, so instead of excusing your sin based on your feelings or personal philosophies, measure yourself against God's standards for holiness.

At other times, if you stray from God's moral standards, you may find yourself Pharisaically rigid about issues that the Lord has given you great freedom in. You don't have to draw a line in the sand where the Lord has given you the whole beach. God's laws are good. They serve to give you the fullest life and protect you from the damage of sin, and they are sufficient in every way just as they are.

As easy as it is to minimize sin or be unnecessarily rigid, you may be even more susceptible to magnify sin's dominance in your life. Do not fall prey to undue self-condemnation. Yes, sin separates you from God, but remember who your God is—he is "merciful and gracious, slow to anger, and abounding in steadfast love and faithfulness" (Ex. 34:6). When faced with your sin, you will often need to remind yourself of your sainthood earned for you through the life, death, and resurrection of Jesus who reconciled you to your God. Who are we to think that Jesus's death was not enough to cover our failings as a person or a parent? Do we think so little of all Christ did for us that we think our sins are greater than his grace? Take great comfort in being a chosen, forgiven, and adopted child of God. Sin will be part of your life, but it will not define who you are in God. Conviction to be sanctified is a holy pursuit, but wallowing in self-condemnation is not Christian.

A major factor of your integrity will be your ability to repent quickly, easily, and thoroughly. You will see in yourself, and others will point out to you, where you have fallen short of being the reliable disciple-maker you are called to be. None of us will walk in perfection before God or before our kids, but you can be reliable in the way you confess and repent of your sin where and when you should. That means you will repent always to God, always to who you sinned against, and often in the witness of your family. You who follow Jesus will repent often, and you will experience profound grace and forgiveness for each other and from God since none of you are perfect. It is all part of your ongoing mission to deny yourself and put sin to death in your life. Though the race for your salvation has already been won in Christ, we run the race of this life fixated on Christlikeness, fighting sin as if to win. We dash with every ounce of effort we can muster to arrive at the finish line to cheers from our heavenly Father crying out with roaring approval, "Well done, good and faithful servant!"

Modeling Requires You to Be Relatable

In order to be a model for your kids you must follow Christ in proximity to your children. Modeling requires a close, loving relationship with those you hope to lead and influence. Be relatable enough to let those close to you see who you really are. Be vulnerable enough to let someone see your life—how you make your choices, how you handle failure, and how you turn to God's word to determine who you are and what you're called to.

Live your life with your kids purposely nearby. Quality proximity is paramount to your effectiveness as a discipling parent. Don't just be in the same room or the same car as your children; be an active participant in their lives. Don't just be a lecturer for your children; help them become your colaboring apprentice. Invite them to observe and participate in your life. Be ready to share with your children not only the gospel of God but also your own self, because they are so very dear to you (1 Thess. 2:8).

Yes, sharing your life with your kids will mean they will get exposed to your shortcomings, but there is a good chance that your greatest failures might be your most relatable and profound lessons. Your kids will be far from perfect too so they need you to demonstrate how a man or woman of God handles pursuing godliness repentantly without wallowing in failure or seeking worldly affirmation to cope. Your kids don't need perfect parents; they need to know how their imperfect family can know and follow their perfect heavenly Father. Don't be afraid to let your kids see you make mistakes, but always glorify God that where we are weak he is strong, and even in the struggles we wish would be behind us, his grace is sufficient for us. Likewise, don't be afraid to let your kids make mistakes themselves. We don't advise letting sin go unchecked, but let them put effort into tasks they may not be able to achieve on their own yet and make decisions they think are wise even if you can already see the consequences they'll soon be facing and learning from. Being relatable means sharing your honest, insufficient life and loving them enough to delight in theirs too.

In order to know their life you have to be in their life. If you are like most parents, you probably see your kids almost every day, but how often do you actually *look* at your kids? You probably hear your kids every day, but do you actually *listen* to them? You should regularly get face-to-face with them and give them the all too rare gift of your *full* attention. Ask for the same in return. Two people can be in the same room, but if their backs are to one another they are twenty-five thousand miles away from looking each other in the eye. Family discipleship modeling requires more than passive proximity. It takes turning toward one another. It takes listening and asking loving follow-up questions that you genuinely want the answers to. It asks you to give your earnest representation of Christian adulthood taught through a sincerely loving relationship. Looking and listening take a great degree of time and care, and that's why they express a genuine love. Let them know you are watching them. Encourage them in the godly traits you see in them.

Your kids probably see you every day, but do they *watch* you? They hear you talk every day, but are you inviting them to *listen* to what you say and how you say it? Encourage them to regurgitate the godly language you use and imitate the godly characteristics they witness in your life. Go before them in living out what you want them to catch from you. If you want your kids to be repentant over their sin, first share where you are experiencing godly grief in your heart and invite them into that vulnerable and honest space with you. You love them. Let them see it manifested in how you spend time with them. Usher your kids into a relationship with you that will help them understand why God asked us to call him Father in the way we relate to him and called us to be imitators of him as dearly loved children (Eph. 5:1).

Christ is the model for your life as well as your kid's life. Remember, you are not Christ. Your imperfect presence is not enough for your kids. Family discipleship is not just "being a Christian near your children." Don't assume your model is enough for children to grasp the gospel. Be tenacious at pointing out *how* and *why* you are choosing to follow Christ. Use your words to intentionally instruct your family in all of the gospel's ramifications in your daily life as well as versing them in the story of God's plan to rescue the world from the problem of sin through Jesus Christ.

Remodeling

Many of you reading this are blazing a new trail of Christian parenting in your family. Many of your generation's parents were not godly role models. It is easy to be embittered or feel shortchanged by thinking about your upbringing, but now it is your generation's turn to try to step up to the call to disciple even if it's a pioneering work for you. If you need it, first ask the Lord to give you a forgiving and humble heart toward your own parents. Second, please know that you are not doomed to repeat the sins of your parents. And equally freeing, your kids are not obligated or destined to revisit your failings that will be surely evident to them.

If you've never had a godly parent role model, it might be wise for you to invite a mentor mom, dad, or couple into your life. Mentoring does not have to be lifelong or taxing. It can be as simple as identifying someone you know whom you could learn from as a parent, inviting him or her to a meal or coffee, and coming ready with questions about family discipleship. You might also ask someone whose kids are a little older than yours if you could sit in and observe some of that family's family discipleship time.

If you never had a Christian life modeled for you at home, you may be at a disadvantage compared to someone who did, but you are not excused from leading the next generation in knowing and obeying all that Christ commanded. Don't let your children have the same disadvantage you are attempting to overcome, an undiscipled childhood. Regardless of your past, your future can be one of care, concern, and contrition for the sake of your kids. Who are you modeling your parenting after? Look to those godly families around you and look to Christ, who serves as the ultimate model in all godliness. You will find in God's word and the life of Christ more than sufficient guidance in who you are to be and what your life is to be about. Your family's legacy of faithfulness can start with you.

Jesus Discipled through Modeling

When it comes to discipleship, the only model worth fully emulating is that of Jesus Christ himself. In the Scriptures you see him love, lead, and serve in every way perfectly. He loved those whom others ignored. He spoke truth even if it was unpopular. He made time to pray regularly. He lived righteously even in the face of temptation. Anyone who lives a Christian life "ought to walk in the same way in which he walked" (1 John 2:6). As he discipled the twelve, he purposely invited them, and by extension you, to follow his example, to copy him.

In John 13, Jesus taught his disciples a lesson on humility and service by washing their feet. He intended this not only to be an object lesson to pull insight from but to be an example for them to follow. "If I then, your Lord and Teacher, have washed your feet, you also ought to wash one another's feet. For I have given you an example, that you also should do just as I have done to you" (John 13:14–15). Along with that invitation comes a promise and a reason. "If you know these things, blessed are you if you do them" (13:17). This is the way you should talk to your kids as you serve them and meet their needs. Explain to your kids why you as a parent meet their needs and invite them to do the same for others that they might experience the same blessing that results from love for one another.

Jesus's discipling ministry serves as a fantastic model for parents to emulate. He exemplifies leading by example. According to Jesus, you are the light of the world. He has called you to deliberately let your light shine before your family, so that they may see your good works and give glory to your Father who is in heaven (Matt. 5:16). Christ is the only person who never had a "love disorder." Your love will be your witness that it is Christ whom you follow. The ministry of Jesus centers on highly prioritized love—so should the ministry of leading your family. As we think about modeling Christlikeness for our children, we must place the highest emphasis on a rightly ordered life of loves.

Love Your Kids by Loving Your God

One of the best ways you can love your child well is by loving your God well. Your kids learn how to love God by watching how you love God. While you are called to disciple your kids, the call is not to give them a fictitiously polished version of yourself. It is essential for the spiritual development of your home that you have a genuine walk with God and a genuinely repentant response to failings. Your relationship with God is fostered through spiritual discipline and rooted in a love of God and others.

Before you can lead your home, you have to follow your God. We make time for what we consider to be important. Looking at how you spend your time can help you assess what you have prioritized. What time in your week is strategically and intentionally given to your relationship with God and your family's relationship with God? What are your spiritual disciplines?

Like any relationship you want to strengthen, it is important to make consistent investments into your relationship with God. If you want to deepen your relationship with particular people, then you ask them questions, listen to them, and act on what they are asking of you. The same things can be said of your relationship with God. What questions are you asking of him as you look to his word or as you pray? Are you growing in knowledge of him? Once you have heard what he has asked of you, what are you doing to act on it?

The Bible is the inspired and perfect word of God. It is trustworthy. God, who knows everything, wrote it to tell you about himself. Its commands are to be obeyed, its story believed, and its promises trusted. For most of you, it is readily available. So how are you spending your time in God's word? Regular interaction with the word of God is an essential element of understanding who your God is, his plan for the world, and your part in it. A vibrant spiritual life, one worth emulating, starts with a life saturated in God's word. But we don't simply read it; we seek to understand how it reads us. The word of God is a useful guide to know how to live, but even more than that, it is a pathway to learning and loving God as well as his promises and plans for you.

Many people struggle with reading and understanding the Bible. First, we can tell you with great certainty that you will never understand the Bible if you don't at least open the cover and read it. We recommend making a resolution to spend designated time studying (not just reading). Also, consider investing in simple Bible commentaries, inductive Bible studies, or reading resources that can guide you through a portion of Scripture.

Prayer goes hand in hand with spending time in Scripture. A strong spiritual life involves pouring out your heart to God. God is attentive and responsive, and he never tires of our prayers regardless of our persistence. God has commanded us to pray because he wants to hear from his people. In Scripture, God commands us to pray to be in relationship with him by praising him, confessing our sins, giving thanks, and interceding for others (Matt. 6:9–13; James 5:16; Phil. 4:4–7). We also make our requests to God in prayer, because though he rules over everything, in a mysterious way God uses prayer to change things. Through prayer, God changes both his people and the world. God is active in every major and minute detail of existence at all times. "This is the confidence that we have toward him, that if we ask anything according to his will he hears us" (1 John 5:14). Praying with, for, and in front of your kids are all important parts of family discipleship modeling. Jesus would often pray alone, but he would also pray with others (Luke 5:16; John 17).

Just as many people struggle with reading and understanding the Bible, many struggle with focused, especially prolonged, prayer. First, prayer does not require special methods or special words since God hears everything we say and think. But certain methods may help you when it comes to your ability to focus. Try writing out your prayers in a journal so that your mind does not wander. This will also enable you to look back and see how the Lord has responded. Praying out loud or praying through a psalm are also helpful strategies to get you started. Don't hesitate to be honest with God about what is difficult about life and about praying in general.

Invite accountability into your life. Share with a friend or mentor the temptations and transgressions you are experiencing. Be honest with others about what is hard, what lies you are believing about God and yourself, what you want to start, and what you want to stop, and give them permission to ask you personal questions and call you out where you need it. Your kids are under your authority. Model for them what it looks like to be a person under authority who humbly seeks to follow wisdom from others and share life's dilemmas with trusted companions.

There are many other ways to habitually realign your heart around God and his commands. You can evaluate your practices of worship, rest, Communion, fasting, evangelism, serving, and engaging in biblical community/accountability. These are practices the Lord has called us to because in them we commune and interact with him. They reorient our lives around what is right, good, and true.

Love Your Kids by Loving Yourself

The Bible calls us to love our neighbors as we love ourselves (Matt. 22:39). Implicit in that command is that Christians should have a godly and honest love for themselves. This is not the call for self-obsession or fixation. Narcissism has no place in the heart of the believer, but neither do self-loathing, self-harm, or self-neglect. Your kids learn to love themselves by watching you love yourself. How you talk about yourself and how you take care of yourself says something to your family.

For many people, there is no one they treat worse than themselves. When you insult yourself, gripe about your shortcomings, or compare yourself unfavorably to someone else, you are teaching your family that what is not okay for someone else to say to or about you is okay for you to say to or about yourself. That is simply not true. If you are in Christ, you are a son or daughter of the King and have been clothed in the righteousness of Jesus. Who are you to insult who God has made you to be or to covet what God made of someone else? Trusting God will mean loving who God made you! Of course we want to be sanctified from where sin has twisted our hearts, minds, and bodies, but sin compounds when we make our shortcomings our identity. To raise kids who understand who and why God made them the way he did, you should demonstrate a thorough refusal to endure disrespect, even from yourself.

Just as detrimental and probably much more common is your instinct as a parent to find your value in who your kids are, what they can do, and how they behave. Love yourself enough to not find your identity in your children's capabilities. When you act like your joy or sorrow rests on the success or failure of your children, you model for your kids that a person's identity is tied to the strengths and weaknesses of his or her progeny. First, no kid can live up to those standards; they cannot be your vicarious accomplishments. Second, a godly self-image will model a Christian confidence regarding who you are; it will display how your self-appraisal and status is not tied to your children or any other human relationship.

Our identity as Christians is firmly rooted in Christ. His love for you is not contingent on your merit. If it were, you would not have it. It does not waver in favor based on your achievements, your appearance, your abilities, or those of your children. How many kids have fallen prey to the diabolical lies of a sliding scale of personal value? Treat yourself as you want your kids to treat themselves, as a beloved child of God who looks to Christ to know who they are and whether they matter.

Love Your Kids by Loving Your Neighbor

Your kids learn how to love their neighbors by watching how you love your neighbors. Jesus called the love of your neighbor the second most important law in the whole of the Bible. This is the mission of the church on earth, to share the gospel with those who don't know Christ and to be the gospel to those who are in need. Jesus tells a parable about a Good Samaritan to clarify that our neighbor love is not to have limits based on our differences. Jesus modeled this love by extending compassion to people from all walks of life. He was kindhearted to the poor, sick, disabled, rejected, ethnically estranged, and notorious sinners.

Jesus serves as our model for how to live a life pursuing the will of God. If we want to be men and women worth following, then we should be men and women constantly loving the marginalized and defending the defenseless. Personal biases are so easy for kids to pick up on, so let us demonstrate for them hearts unencumbered by sinful prejudices against people who are different from us.

Humans do not have a sliding scale of value based on wealth, health, history, or ethnicity. As James instructs, "Show no partiality as you hold the faith in our Lord Jesus Christ, the Lord of glory" (James 2:1). Few aspects of the Christian life are better to model for your kids than selfless, impartial service to others. Serving is not only how we lead and how we express God's love for others; it also flies in the face of the sinful instincts of our selfish hearts. Kids left to their own devices will not desire to consider others before themselves, so model it and invite them into it. Serving our neighbors cultivates gratitude, empathy, and love, and it counteracts entitlement.

Love Your Kids by Loving Your Spouse

If you are married, one of the best ways that you can love your child well is by loving your spouse well. Imagine the power of your example of Christlike love for your spouse in the eyes and ears of your children! According to the Bible your marriage is a demonstration of the gospel, the relationship between Christ and the church (Eph. 5:22–23). Your marriage can be how your kids learn about the sacrificial love of Christ. Put the unconditional love of God on display by working on loving your spouse like God loves you, a love not based on merit, a love that does not keep score. It is part of how your kids will know how Christ loves them.

Keep in mind that as you parent, you aren't just trying to shape godly children; you are helping grow God-fearing adults. Your kids might be husbands and fathers or wives and mothers themselves one day, and they will take their cues from their experience with your example on how best to be that. Set an example, not only in how to lead a family but how to love someone more than yourself. We have seen many homes where the kids became more important than the marriage, where life became primarily about meeting the needs of the kids, and the husband and wife stopped considering each other's needs. Do not neglect your marriage in the false name of loving your kids.

It is good for your kids to see that you love your spouse differently than you love them and that you put your relationship with your spouse first. It is good for your kids to see you take your spouse on a date—to sit together, to sacrifice for one another, to surprise, serve, and delight in each other. It is good for your kids to hear you consistently speak well of each other. Let the love for your spouse always be the predominant human love in your house. If your love for your kids starts to become the priority over your spouse, you actually do everyone a disservice. Your marriage is a lifelong covenant, and it takes work and focus. And while you will hopefully know and love your kids your whole life, your relationship with your children should always be progressing toward a launch day. There is a reason that one day children will leave their father and mother and cleave to another or become independent as an adult operating under their own authority.

Consider your marital spiritual life. How can you and your spouse pursue God together more intimately? Will you study the word or do devotions together? Will you have a shared committed prayer life? Will you fast together? What will be your shared spiritual disciplines? In the Griffin home, early in our marriage we established Our Hour. My wife and I marked our calendar to spend an hour a week talking about our spiritual lives and catching up with each other. It is easy to see each other and hear from each other every day, but Our Hour was our chance to actually *look* at each other and *listen* to each other.

Be careful to love your spouse without putting your spouse in the place where only God should be in your life. Since a spouse is a good thing, it is easy to twist him or her into being your ultimate thing. The pleasure and preferences of your husband or wife must still be subservient to that of your true God. If you find that you are serving your spouse as your idol or that your emotional health rests fully on how your spouse is feeling about you, then you desperately need to realign your life around Christ.

Conclusion

Family discipleship modeling is serving as a godly example for your family, living out your genuine walk with God, and demonstrating true repentance where and when you fall short.

Kids learn from how you live. God has asked you to be diligent in the way that you care for your own soul, and he wants you to invite your children to follow your example as you follow Christ. Teach your kids that everyone desperately needs Jesus, including you as you experience forgiveness and grace for your sin. In order to set an example worth following you should be both reliable and relatable for your children— a person of repentant integrity in relational proximity to your family. Serve as a godly example, living out your genuine walk with God and demonstrating true repentance where and when you fall short.

Questions

Answer these on your own or, if you're married, with your spouse, and make a plan for your own spiritual disciplines that will help you model a genuine walk with God.

1. If a stranger took a look at your weekly schedule or read a transcript of every word you said in a day, what do you think they would guess are the most important things in your life?

2. Describe how a "walk with God" was or wasn't modeled for you in your own upbringing.

3. List some things that you would like to see reproduced and repeated in your kid's childhood from your own upbringing. Then list what you would like to see redeemed or changed for the better.

4. Make a list of the inconsistencies you can see between what you tell your kids is right and what they see you do.

5. Read Deuteronomy 4:9 and 6:4–9. Take note of the things God calls us to do "diligently." *Diligent* describes a strong commitment to something. In other words, we work hard and don't give up easily.

   What do you think it looks like to "care for your own soul"? How can you care for your soul diligently? What do you think it should look like to "teach your children" diligently?

6. Our kids learn from how we live. Read Galatians 5:19–26 and think about what you are struggling with now or what you struggled with in the past that you don't want to model to your kids.

7. What spiritual habits and fruit of the Spirit would you like to see developed in your kids that you want to work on modeling? When/how could you do that?

8. If your son or daughter asked you, "What's the difference between someone who is a Christian and someone who isn't?" how would you respond? What Scriptures would you share to help answer this question?

9. Take a couple minutes and consider your personal rhythm of spiritual disciplines. What are the biggest challenges you face when it comes to the following:

   • Personal Bible study
   • Worship
   • Rest
   • Prayer
   • Fasting
   • Generosity
   • Evangelism
   • Solitude
   • Confession
   • Serving
   • Discipling
   • Engaging in biblical community and accountability

10. When can/do you have protected times set aside for intentional personal spiritual development?

11. Who are you quickest to confess to when you mess up and who helps you fight temptation? How can you improve/create some accountability relationships in your life?

12. Good mentors practice three easy steps in training an apprentice. First, they invite a protégé to watch them do something. Second, when they are ready, they do it together. Finally, when appropriate, they let the apprentice do it alone as the mentor evaluates. They *demonstrate, participate,* and *evaluate.* What are some skills or habits in your Christian walk that you could focus on as you mentor your child?

13. If you are married, a great way to love your kids well is to love your spouse well. Take a few minutes to consider your rhythm of practices that promote spousal spiritual intimacy. What are the biggest challenges you face when it comes to the following:

    • Sincere intercession (praying for your spouse)
    • Praying together with your spouse
    • Practicing confession and repentance
    • Sharing your hopes, dreams, and vision for your family
    • Giving permission for feedback
    • Asking each other thought-provoking questions
    • Creating space for intimacy
    • Studying the Bible or a book together
    • Offering encouragement and affirmations
    • Serving one another
    • Serving with one another

14. If you are married, when can/do you have protected times set aside for intentional spousal spiritual development?

15. If you are married and your spouse is not a Christian, what are some ways that you can humbly and respectfully model spiritual development

in your home? Who can join you and support you in seeking the salvation of your household?

It is important to remember that we are talking about working in healthy rhythms; we are not trying to condemn or heap guilt on anyone for what may be lacking. Remember that growth is gradual. We should be diligent but also patient. Spiritual development is more like a marathon than a sprint. Also, it's great to be creative and have fun with how you plan to care for your spiritual health in your home, so take some time to consider designing spiritual activities you'll enjoy.

Using figure 1, Spiritual Disciplines Plan, design what you'd like a typical week to look like for your spiritual disciplines. These might be things like daily quiet times, a meeting with an accountability partner, a church service, an evangelistic meal, or a weekly fast. If you're married, include what you'd like intentional spousal spiritual disciplines to look like. These might be things like date nights, a time of morning prayer, or an hour set aside for spiritually checking in with one another.

Example Spiritual Disciplines Plan

	MORNING	AFTERNOOON	EVENING
S	· Pray and study the Bible		
M	· Pray and study the Bible		
T	· Pray and study the Bible		· Meet with Home group
W	· Pray and study the Bible	· Fast and pray during lunch break	
T	· Pray and study the Bible		
F	· Pray and study the Bible		· Spiritual check-in with spouse
S	· Pray and study the Bible · Meet with mentor or accountability partner for breakfast		

Fig. 1

Spiritual Disciplines Plan

	MORNING	AFTERNOOON	EVENING
S			
M			
T			
W			
T			
F			
S			

"Train up a child in the way he should go; even when he is old he will not depart from it." —Proverbs 22:6

"In matters of doctrine, you will find orthodox congregations frequently change to heterodoxy in the course of thirty or forty years, and that is because too often there has been no catechizing of the children in the essential doctrines of the Gospel."[1] —Charles Spurgeon

"I cannot read the Word, I cannot sing, I cannot pray, without leaving some trace on the tender mind. How solemnly, how affectionately, how believingly, should I then approach this ordinance! With how much godly fear and preparation!"[2] —J. W. Alexander

"If parents are looking for a convenient time to schedule family worship, they may as well forget about the idea. Christianity is not a matter of convenience; it involves cost."[3] —Howard Hendricks

"This world is not our home. Hard things happen. Storms will come. But I love to see God equipping His little ones with His promises from the very beginnings of their lives, helping them know He is with them, helping them recognize Him coming to them."[4] —Sally Lloyd-Jones

"First, as touching the spiritual state of his family, he should be very diligent . . . doing his utmost endeavor both to increase faith where it is begun, and to begin it where it is not. For this reason, he should diligently and frequently lay before his household such things of God out of His Word, as are suitable for each particular."[5] —John Bunyan

4

Time

Family Discipleship Time: Creating intentional time built into the rhythm of the family's life for the purpose of thinking about, talking about, and living out the gospel.

Calendars and clocks have become gods to many in our culture. If not you, then surely someone you know is enslaved by their schedule. When you can't do what you *should* be doing because you feel compelled to do something less important that you believe you *have* to do, you might have a disordered relationship with your itinerary. Or maybe you have the opposite problem; maybe you don't use your time wisely and prefer to waste your time by dedicating it to tasks with no beneficial or eternal significance. Is your life one of fruitless leisured self-indulgence? Perhaps you ignore what the Bible says about "making the best use of the time, because the days are evil" (Eph. 5:16).

As you read through this chapter, consider how you might find daily, weekly, or monthly opportunities to get your family talking about and living out the gospel together. In order to digest what we have to say about family discipleship time, you have to first believe that your clock and your calendar exist to serve you, not the other way around, and that your time is a precious commodity to be invested wisely. In addition, you will have to accept that what we are talking about should jump to the top of your priority list, if it is not already there. When you try to squeeze in some time for family discipleship between other commitments and are distracted by everything else you have going on, or if you make lazy passing attempts at discipling your children, flying by the seat of your pants, whisper to yourself this reminder as you gather your family: "This is exactly where you are supposed to be and this is exactly what you are supposed to be doing, so be all here right now with your family and give it everything you've got."

Family discipleship time is the regular gathering of your family for time in God's word, in prayer, in worship, in conversation, and in living out the calls of Scripture. It is the base strength of your overall discipling strategy. It can be semisporadic or every day. It can be always changing or stable for decades, but what your family discipleship time cannot be is nonexistent.

Family devotions, family worship, Bible story time—whatever you want to call it, it's an integral ingredient in family discipleship. While the timing and regularity might be different for every family and even shift as families enter different life stages, every Christian family should have some regular time to meet where the main purpose is spiritual growth.

This is your family's foundation as well as reinforcement for discipleship, the bones that lend structure and organization to the meat of your children's training. But if you read this and fearfully think that your family must sit for thirty to sixty minutes in a circle in perfect, attentive bliss as you expound some deep theological tenet to their eager ears, please lower your expectations. While that may be your experience, more likely you will have a partially attentive, often resistant, and distracted audience that can manage a few minutes at a time of structured family devotions. Fight to get whatever you can, but let yourself off the hook for having a perfectly executed long-form exhortation that always leaves your family wanting more. It is important to have realistic expectations, but not to give up altogether just because it may be less than perfect.

Building time in God's word together into your family's rhythms is one of the most critical aspects of family discipleship. Whatever you teach your children should be backed up by and saturated in the word of God. Do you believe that the Bible is the word of God? If the answer is yes, have you read it? If the answer is "some of it," then you are like many others among us who claim Christ. We are glad you are reading this book, but when it comes to leading your home, reading and knowing the heart of God as he recorded it in his word is better by far. Our words and your words will pass away but his never will. Paul calls the Bible "sacred writings, which are able to make you wise for salvation through faith in Christ Jesus" (2 Tim. 3:15).

The word of God shows us who God is, it shows us who we are, and it shows us how we are to line our lives up with how God designed the universe to work. The word of God beckons you to come and have a relationship with God regardless of your current situation. The word of God is going to kick down the door of your heart, lay your family bare, discerning your family members' thoughts and intentions (Heb. 4:12) and showing you the motives behind your actions. The Bible is "breathed out by God and profitable for teaching, for reproof, for correction, and for training in righteousness, that the man of God may be complete, equipped for every good work" (2 Tim. 3:16–17).

God's word is wisdom to a people who would otherwise be susceptible to the dangers of leaning on their own understanding (Prov. 3:5–6). It teaches us and reminds us what God promises. When Paul writes, "Children, obey your parents in the Lord, for this is right," he is talking directly to kids (Eph. 6:1). He is assuming that children will be reading or hearing the word of God directly, not waiting to read or hear the Bible until they are considered adults. Family discipleship time is time *right now* to show your children what God has to say to them *right now*.

Teaching God's word to your children does not require a seminary degree. You do not have to be a theology wizard to lead your family. You can do this! In fact, you can teach your home about God as *you* learn about God. Spending personal time in his word, listening attentively to sermons, navigating a catechism, and learning from other related resources can be a great lead-in to how you coach your family. What God is teaching you right now might be what he is equipping you to teach right now. You only have to be one step ahead on a path in order to show someone which way to go. You can even learn *together* as you read a few verses and ask simple questions like, "If this is true, what does it change about us and how we live our lives?"

Don't underestimate what your kids can learn and memorize. From a very young age, kids are capable of memorizing Scripture and repeating catechism answers verbatim. A catechism is a resource designed to teach orthodox Christian doctrine in the form of questions and answers. A good catechism will teach the Ten Commandments, creeds, prayers, or theological tenets in a format that is easy to navigate. There are many options to choose from that can assist you and your children in learning the truths of God, comprehending them, and committing them to memory.

Prayer must also play a central role in your family discipleship time. Your family can talk to God together. It is not complex or formal. It's simply interacting with God: praising him, thanking him, confessing sin, and asking him for what you need using everyday plain language. It doesn't take special words or special lengths of time. Though you probably know you should pray together and that it doesn't have to be complicated, almost all of us would say, "I'm a believer in Christ, I know I should pray, and I know how to pray, but I find my prayer life lacking." Knowing we "should" tends to lead to guilt as a motivator. We don't pray with our families out of guilt over forsaken duty or out of intimidation of a demanding God we've assumed is hypercritical. We pray because we *need* God and we have been invited into his presence to commune with him. When it comes to prayer, one of Jesus's motivations in teaching people was that they would "not lose heart" (Luke 18:1).

Bible study and prayer are not the only ways of gathering your family around God's truth. Every family benefits from finding opportunities to live out the gospel together. Deployment is an important aspect of family discipleship. Family discipleship isn't just about learning Jesus's words; it's about practicing his ways. Following Christ can not be relegated to small group or individual study, and training does not happen only through a lecture. When it comes to serving others, sharing the gospel, and making disciples of others, we want our kids to "graduate" from our homes being able to say "I've done that before" and not just "I remember hearing about this." Training children through family discipleship time requires not only study, but plenty of exercise. Family discipleship time is an opportunity to practice the "one anothers" of the Bible and not just memorize and study them. Think about the needs that your family can address in your community side by side. Family practice looks like your family serving and sharing the gospel together.

Family discipleship time is about cultivating spiritual maturity in your household through loving, gospel-centered relationships and appointed times. Although formal teaching can certainly play a significant role, it isn't exclusively about that. It's planned time that is dedicated to the spiritual growth of your family. You may utilize rhythms and gathering points that already exist in your household, like going to church services together, eating a meal together, commuting to school or work, getting ready for the day, or getting ready for bed. You might also want to establish a new rhythm, like a family game night, serving through a local nonprofit, a family Bible study, or a family service project. If major changes are needed in your family in order to start meeting together, they are changes worth making.

You will face resistance from your children sometimes, maybe often. They will not want to gather as a family to talk about or live out the things of God. You cannot force your kids to become believers, but in your hopes that they would be, you can make family discipleship a nonnegotiable. As hard as it might be, this is a hill to die on. With all grace and gentleness, consider making family discipleship time sacred and mandatory. Being a part of your family should mean being a part of regular gospel-centered gathering.

In Our Homes

In the Chandler house, our rhythms of family discipleship time are more varied than they are uniform. They change based on the season of the year or the season of life. During Lent, we have family conversations and updates on what we have given up for the season as we consider Christ's sacrifice. During Advent, we count down the days until Christmas with various related Scripture readings. For most of the year, family devotions happen about once a week, and they are usually planned during a meeting my wife and I have every Sunday night to talk about our budget, calendar, and what's going on with the kids.

While most family discipleship times for the Chandlers are unremarkable, at times we've stretched ourselves creatively. Once we turned our living room into a gargantuan fort. We must have used every blanket from every bed in our house and all the pillows in our living room to build a giant, indoor fortress. Then we climbed inside, opened our Bible, and talked about how God is our strong tower. We had a great conversation about what that means for the Chandlers.

It would be hard to do something like that every day, but there are easier things we can do (that require much less cleanup) to regularly get in touch with God and our kid's hearts. A more frequent part of our family rhythm is a game we call Low/High, which is built around our family meal. At a Chandler family dinner we go around our dining room table and give each family member time to talk about his or her least favorite part of the day and the most favorite part of the day. Not only do we learn what's going on with each other, but we often enter into spiritual conversations about what delights and what bothers us. It requires very little preparation, and it yields great results.

But not all of our regular family discipleship times are this informal. Some take more planning. My wife and my oldest daughter, who is now a teenager, get together one-on-one once a week to read through a book of the Bible together. My teenage son and I get together weekly too in order to study and pray. Right now, we are reading through some Proverbs and answering questions about them. Then we go through a grid of questions related to friends, girls, sin, and sports. I also ask him what he thinks his mom and I could be doing better as parents. These regular rhythms of spiritual conversation, whether it's an appointment on the calendar or around some regular family rhythms like our meals, are some of the most important investments we make in our kids.

The kids in the Griffin home are still in elementary school so our most regular family discipleship times have not changed since our kids were born. Our times are built around our bedtime routine, so almost every night before we say goodnight we follow a simple ritual of reading, sharing, singing, and praying together. We start by reading a story from the Bible. Now that our kids can all have deeper conversations, we follow that up with some applications and questions about the text. Then we all put our hands in the middle, and one or two of us prays. As our kids have gotten older, we have begun to assign them to pray and to ask for prayer requests. Then we all hold hands and sing a song, usually a benediction song or the doxology. As we conclude our family discipleship time, we hug each boy individually and recite a "life verse" that we chose for each one of them. These verses are their first to memorize, and they summarize some of our hopes for their lives.

We look our oldest, Oscar, in the eye and say, "Be watchful, stand firm in the faith, act like men, be strong. Let all that you do be done in love" (1 Cor. 16:13–14). For Gus it is King David's last words to his son and heir, King Solomon: "Be strong, and show yourself a man, and keep the charge of the LORD your God, walking in his ways and keeping his statutes" (1 Kings 2:2–3). For Theodore, our youngest, we ask, "He has told you, O man, what is good; / and what does the LORD require of you / but to do justice, and to love kindness, and to walk humbly with your God?" (Mic. 6:8). Then it's lights out and goodnight.

The Two Key Components of Time

In order to have a sustainable practice of family gospel gatherings you will need to incorporate both a consistent rhythm and intentionality.

- *Rhythm:* Be steady, designating the times with commitment and consistency.
- *Intentionality:* Be studied, designing the times with planning and purpose.

Family Discipleship Time Requires a Consistent Rhythm

Exercising can help make a body stronger and faster, but only if you do it with discipline and consistency. The same is true for the spiritual strength of your family. One-off occasional family devotions are good, but they will not have the same positive cumulative effect on your child's training as gatherings done consistently. Family discipleship time should be something religiously habitual for your household. We recommend that spiritual leadership times be woven into what you're already doing, rather than adding more to your schedule. It is up to you to designate when your family will meet.

Your family has a lot of rhythms. Work, sleep, school, play, showers, church, brushing teeth, haircuts, and more all happen in the context of your family's ordinary rhythm. Time spent in God's word together best occurs as a normal part of everyday life for your household. It should not feel like a departure from the norm to have appointed spiritual conversations with each other. Of course, if this is a new rhythm for you, it may feel awkward or clunky at first, but persevere and it will soon be as natural a part of your life as everything else your family is used to. Deuteronomy 6 asks you to be diligent in telling your kids these things. Diligent means you don't give up. Diligent means you are patient. Diligent means you don't compromise the truth just because it might make your child uncomfortable. Consistency reinforces the truths you are teaching. No human being, regardless of age, learns something by being told once, and then never again. We teach over and over and over again. Getting it right the first time does not mean you're done; it means you have opportunity for repetition. We diligently have conversations again and again. Consistency breeds clarity.

Whatever works for your family—be it daily or weekly meetings or something slightly more irregular, ten minutes at a go or an hour—it will take diligence and discipline to maintain it. The wherewithal required to sustain a regimen of meeting, especially when you face resistance, can be pretty mammoth. This is why it is essential that you understand the level of priority family discipleship time should have in your life and the strength and love of the God who empowers you for it. If you do not grasp how important this time is, you will easily find reasons to put it off, to quit, or to invest less than your best. Make family discipleship time normal. Doing your unique best at making these times happen regularly will be an important part of your faith legacy. Be relentlessly consistent.

The easiest way to be consistent is to attach family discipleship time to something you are already doing. Utilize your bedtime routine, your commute, grocery shopping, a breakfast before school, lunch after church, or a regular family movie/game night to engage in spiritual conversations.

Family Discipleship Time Requires Intentionality

You don't start construction on a new home unless you have some blueprints. Every step of the process is guided by those plans. The foundation, studs, and bricks need to not only be put in the right place but built in the right order. The goal is clear: build a house. But accomplishing the goal requires great energy and intentionality to do it right. If you want to build a strong family, you will need a plan, and if you want to communicate that plan, you'll need to prioritize connecting. Project teams that fail to purposefully meet tend to drift from the plan. It's the same with every family. It's up to you to design the times you gather.

Some parents believe, or at least operate as if they believe, that the discipleship of their kids will happen "naturally" or "organically." Unfortunately, what they often mean is that their parenting philosophy involves expecting their kids to pick up sufficient spiritual wisdom and guidance without the parents themselves having to lend much deliberate leadership or thoughtfulness to the process. If you have ever seen the difference between a garden left to grow naturally and one that is tended, you know that an untended garden is a wild mess of weeds or a shriveled lifeless desert. If your kids are left to grow "naturally," their lives are much more likely to look like a vice-ridden thicket than a virtuous spiritual vineyard. In the same manner that a garden is nurtured with loving attention continually—removing the weeds, watering the roots, and pruning the branches—the spiritual maturity of your family should be well considered, calculated, and cultivated deliberately. Those hoping to start an orchard best do more than throw some apple cores into a field and cross their fingers. Regular time together centered around God will not just happen. You will have to make time for gospel conversations.

Some versions of family discipleship are more spontaneous, and we'll discuss those in the next chapter as we discuss family discipleship moments, but family discipleship time is different. It is proactive, not passive. It is planned. It is not impromptu. You don't stumble upon a chance to serve or study together on a regular basis. It will require purposeful premeditation.

Intentionality will also require personal investment. Think honestly, Who is getting your utmost? Where do you expend your best efforts? You'd never think of coming in to work late or cutting corners on a presentation to a big client, but many of us will wing it when it comes to the spiritual leadership of our homes. Many parents consider their occupations a great service to their family, which they are, but sometimes what we do for a living to provide for our family also deprives our families of our presence and attention. Someone has to win. Being intentional doesn't require much. Give even ten minutes of your week to planning and praying about what family discipleship time could look like, and you'll see the fruit that having purpose brings to your home.

Jesus Planned Discipleship Times

Jesus was not just a model for his disciples; he also consistently and intentionally taught them. Many of his lessons came in the form of sermons, parables, and teachings. He taught different-sized groups at different times across a variety of topics and venues. Formal teaching at appointed times was a normal part of Jesus's ministry.

In Matthew 5–7 he taught a large crowd on the side of a mountain in what is known as the Sermon on the Mount. In Matthew 10 he commissioned his disciples for the work of ministry. In Matthew 13:1–53, he sat down in a boat by the sea and taught a group of followers through parables. In John 3:1–21 he had a small, intimate meeting to talk theology with one man named Nicodemus, a man of the Pharisees. In Matthew 28:16, the disciples went to meet the resurrected Jesus at a place and time he had told them about. This is where he gave them the Great Commission. According to Luke 22:39, it was customary for Jesus to go the Mount of Olives to pray with his disciples. At their request, he taught his disciples how to pray in Luke 11:1–13. In Luke 4:14–30, we see that part of Jesus's routine was to go to a synagogue on the Sabbath, and sometimes he would even get up to teach from the word of God himself.

Many of Jesus's teachings were steeped in the words of the Old Testament. It was expected that from childhood, Jewish families would teach their children God's word. Timothy, one of Paul's disciples, had been trained by his mother and grandmother to know the scriptures. Paul points out to Timothy the legacy of faith he'd inherited:

"I am reminded of your sincere faith, a faith that dwelt first in your grandmother Lois and your mother Eunice and now, I am sure, dwells in you as well" (2 Tim. 1:5). Paul tells him to "continue in what you have learned and have firmly believed, knowing from whom you learned it and how from childhood you have been acquainted with the sacred writings, which are able to make you wise for salvation through faith in Christ Jesus" (2 Tim. 3:14–15). May your legacy be similar. You cannot passively train your children in the way they should go. They will not pick up on the doctrine of God by instinct. Be more than their caretaker. Be their teacher.

Teaching Your Family

Telling your kids something is nowhere near the same thing as teaching your kids something. Mark Twain is credited with saying, "If teaching were the same as telling, we'd all be so smart we could hardly stand it." In other words, people tell each other a lot of things and consider that to be something taught or learned, but just because you tell your kids something does not mean they have learned it. This is as true in behavior as it is in sports, as it is in academics, as it is in spiritual matters. You can't teach someone to play the French horn by showing them a picture of one and telling them, theoretically, about how it would work if they had one. You can read all you want about how to do it and listen to hours of French horns playing, but you still have not been taught until you've tried it yourself and coupled instruction with evaluated practice. If you want to be a great teacher and trainer for your family, then it will require thoughtfulness with your methods.

There's a big difference between *telling* and *teaching* when it comes to imparting truth to your children from the word of God. In *telling* the parent is thinking, "What am I going to say?," where as in *teaching* the parent is considering, "How can I help my child understand this?" In *telling* parents asks their children questions like "Do you understand?" and "Does that make sense?" and are looking for a head nod.

In *teaching* a parent is asking things like "Can you explain that to me?" and "What do I mean when I say . . . ?" in order to evaluate their children's grasp of what's being taught and to get them to interact with the content. A positive result from *telling* is that children remember some of what the parents said, but a positive result from *teaching* goes beyond regurgitation to the ability to demonstrate, distinguish, and defend what they've been taught.

Planning family discipleship time can first seem like it requires a lot of work, but if you are an effective teacher, the strategy should be squarely pointed at forcing your children to be the ones who are working through the content and practicing its implications for themselves, not you *for* them. This is how people learn best. You don't want them to just remember the true things you say; you want to find a way to lead them to the point where a true conclusion comes out of their own mouths without you having to put it there. Your goal is not just to feed them from the word of God, but to teach them how to feed themselves. You are training them to not need you, but to recognize how they will always desperately need God.

Every family would be served by a clear "scope and sequence." Scope is everything you want to cover and sequence is when and in what order. Many resources and curricula are designed to help you with family discipleship time content. There are several great catechisms, family devotionals, and various tools designed for different life stages that are both topical and scriptural. However, the best curriculum for your family will always be the Bible itself. Whatever you do, make sure that it is God's word that your family is feeding from. Reading and talking about the Bible can be as simple as choosing a portion of text and then asking some questions. Consider the spiritual maturity level and mental capacity of each member of your family and plan accordingly. Depending on the cognitive ability or age of your children, you may have to accommodate your teaching by asking lower- or higher-level questions as you teach them God's word.

Here are some examples of lower-level questions you might ask as you study the Bible together. These are the kind of things you'll ask after reading a section of Scripture together.

- What did I say about _____?
- How many_____ were mentioned?
- What is _____? *or* What is the definition of _____?
- What do you think about _____?
- Tell me about _____.
- Share an example of _____ from your own experience.
- Explain why _____.

If your kids are a little older or are ready for some higher-level questions, you can use some of these examples below related to a section of the Bible you read together.

- How will this change the way you _____?
- How does _____ apply to you?
- How can you demonstrate or practice _____ in your life?
- If someone said to you, _____, how would you respond?
- What is the difference between _____ and _____?
- Which of these is true, _____ or _____?
- Where do _____ and _____ agree, and where do they differ?
- Which of these is the best course of action and why?
- Make up a metaphor to explain _____.
- Share your vision for what _____ would look like in our family.
- Using your own original words, restate _____.
- Come up with a plan to address _____.
- What makes _____ better than _____?
- What are the advantages and disadvantages of _____?
- What does it look like for our family or you individually to follow Christ in what we read?

Keep It Fun and Simple

One of the most important aspects of your leadership in these family discipleship times will be your intentional application of creativity. You don't want family discipleship time to be the biggest drag on your family's time together; you want it to be the highlight. As you plan, ask yourself the question, "How can we have fun together in family discipleship time this week?" What your family loves to do together might be the best way to build this time into your family's rhythm. If you love arts and crafts, create something in conjunction with your lesson. If you love to watch sports, maybe halftime is a "locker room" family discipleship time. If you love to eat together, maybe you could do devotions while you eat or cook something delicious. If you love movies, pull some scriptural truth from a movie you watch together, and talk about its application. If you love being outside, do family discipleship time in the park, while you walk, or on a boat. If you want to spice up a simple Bible narrative with young kids, act it out or make silly mistakes your kids need to correct. When Jesus discipled, he was often out and about; it was not in a classroom, and it was likely never boring.

It's easy to keep it fun if you keep it simple, and family discipleship time can definitely be simple. Consider this basic formula: Scripture, Share, Song, and Prayer. First, choose a verse or section of Scripture. It could be one verse or it could be a whole story. Ask some questions about what you read, and share what it has to do with your life. For older kids, ask them to read ahead of time and come to family discipleship time with some prepared thoughts and questions. Sing a song from church. Singing is one of the easiest ways to leave scriptural truth echoing in the life of your children, and it's not just for small kids either. Don't underestimate the power of singing with your adolescents. Lastly, pray together. Maybe before you begin, you can talk about the needs of each person present and the needs of extended family and friends. You can all pray, or rotate who prays. You can do this while you eat, get ready for bed, or as you move about your city. It's simple and easy to remember.

Family discipleship time isn't limited to those times when your whole family is gathered together. If you are in a house with multiple kids, you want to take time to look at and listen to each one individually. Focusing on one kid can make a world of difference in sharing each other's hearts and lives. With younger kids you can simply pick a night of the week when one child gets to stay up later than the rest for a special time with Mom and Dad. If your kids are older, you could pick a morning each week or each month for breakfast together to talk about what is going on in each other's lives and what you are learning from the Lord.

Simple and fun! You can definitely do this without making it harder than it needs to be. Family discipleship time should be some of the sweetest and most regular memories in a young child's mind. How criminal if our family discipleship time is so dry that our kids dread it.

Ideas for Family Discipleship Time

Reading through the list of ideas in this chapter can be exciting or it can be intimidating. In your mind and heart, actively work against any feelings of discouragement or anxiety about "opportunities lost" or "one more thing" to put on your calendar.

Daily Family Discipleship Time Ideas

- *Family Meals.* Plan certain meals that you can share and even cook and clean up together. Pray together and guide the mealtime conversation toward the gospel and Scripture. You could even add a reading/memorization or family devotional to breakfast or dinner.
- *Family Prayer.* At some point in the day—first thing in the morning, last thing at night, or on your drive to or from work/school—pray together.

- *Bedtime Routine.* If you have younger children, gather them together before bedtime to read a Bible story. Choose a verse to pray over or with your children as you say goodnight.
- *Family Commute.* As you drive the kids to school or activities, leverage your time in the car to sing together, pray together, or talk about how your family would like to see the gospel lived out today.

Weekly Family Discipleship Time Ideas

- *Family Night.* Plan a night that involves family, food, fun, and your faith.

  - *Movie Night.* Watch something together that could spark conversations while you eat popcorn, pizza, or ice cream. Most movies have a theme of rescue, heroism, sacrifice, friendship, redemption, or evil being defeated or converted. Use these as jumping-off points for a conversation about the gospel.
  - *Game Night.* Play a board game, a card game, or a sport together, and then spend some time encouraging each other in the fruit you see the Spirit growing in each other, such as patience, kindness, self-control, or joy.
  - *Restaurant Night.* Take the family out for dinner and talk about what the Lord is doing in your lives. Seek opportunities to live out your faith in public, to love your server or the people you encounter while you are out.

- *Worship Service.* Go to church services together and discuss what you remember or learned from the teaching after.
- *Family Bible Study/Devotions/Worship.* Pick a devotional study, catechism, or book of the Bible or write some family discipleship questions based on your pastor's sermon and study them together. Ask each other application questions related to the text. Sing worship songs together. Pray.

- *Community.* Attend church small group or another form of biblical community with other families gathering together for the purpose of mutual edification, encouragement, and accountability.
- *Weekly Family Traditions.* In general, consider anything that your family does on a regular basis and think about how you might intentionally design the time for family discipleship. This could be just about anything: watching your favorite show or sports team together, doing yard work, grocery shopping, laundry, and so on.

Monthly Family Discipleship Time Ideas

- *Service.* Find somewhere you can serve together on a regular basis. This could be serving a meal at a homeless shelter, helping a neighbor with housework, or serving on your church's greeting team together.
- *One-on-One Time.* Make time for one parent to take out one child individually—to a movie, to a meal, or anything fun and special to that child. If you have more than one child, have a night of the week or month where one of your children receives complete and caring attention from you. Maybe you can let one of your kids stay up a little later for some special, focused time, or you can do something special on the same day each month, like a note, a gift, or an activity.
- *Guys' Night or Girls' Night.* Have the boys of the family do something with Dad or the girls with Mom on a regular basis to encourage and discuss biblical masculinity or femininity. Moms should engage with sons and dads with daughters in these discussions too. Each brings a unique perspective to these conversations. If you're a single parent, consider how your biblical community might help you with this.
- *Neighborhood Party.* Have your neighbors/friends over regularly to foster a ministry of hospitality and evangelism with your kids.

Conclusion

Family discipleship time is creating intentional time built into the rhythm of the family's life for the purpose of thinking about, talking about, and living out the gospel. Regularly gathering your family around the study and practice of the word of God should be one of your highest calendar priorities. Being consistent and purposeful in how you initiate those times will take some initial planning but the habit of gathering will gain momentum and effectiveness the more ordinary and familiar it becomes. Take stock of what takes up your time and energy, and make sure that family discipleship time is getting some of your foremost attention.

Questions

1. What personal relationship has had the most significant spiritual impact on your life? What was your time together like?

2. On a scale of one to three, rate how much time and consideration your family gives to the following activities. Note: If you are looking at this with someone else, it is okay to have differing opinions and preferences on many of these things.

   1 = Not enough time and consideration
   2 = The right amount of time and consideration
   3 = Too much time and consideration

   __ All family members have time to themselves.
   __ The whole family does something fun together.
   __ The whole family has an in-depth conversation together.
   __ We have fun spending time with people outside the family.
   __ We talk about the gospel together.
   __ We serve or worship together.
   __ The whole family eats meals together.
   __ The parent(s) plan(s) time for when the family will be together.
   __ We work out, participate in activities/hobbies, and/or play sports.

___ We work at our job(s).

___ We sleep.

___ We watch TV, read, play video games, and/or listen to music.

___ We build relationships with those who don't know Christ.

___ We spend time with our biblical community.

___ We manage conflict in a healthy way.

___ If married: My spouse and I have time for just the two of us, without kids.

3. Now that you have finished the exercise above, consider both the downtimes and the busy times of your household. What are the first words that come to mind? Where do you see healthy or unhealthy tendencies? Is there anything you would like to change?

4. When you think about your family's typical week, what rhythms do you identify? What are your gathering points when/where you are together?

5. Is there intentional time built into the rhythm of your family for discipleship? When? Where does it fall on your list of importance? Where should it be on that list?

6. Read Deuteronomy 6:4–9. Looking more closely at verse 7, where do you see those times in your family's rhythm? Where are you intentionally and regularly talking about the things of God with your family?

7. In a busy house, it may be easier to be more purposeful with the time you already have than to add a new family gathering. Is there more you could do to take advantage of your family's time together for thinking about, talking about, and living out the gospel? How can increasing intentionality and planning in your current family gatherings make them better?

8. If your son or daughter asked you, "Why are we doing this?" how would you explain your hopes and goals for family discipleship time?

9. What times of your day, week, or month could you dedicate to family discipleship? How often will you do them? (What's your rhythm?)

10. What could help you keep the commitment to family discipleship times so that they are consistent, thoughtful, and intentional? Who will know your plan and hold you accountable by asking you about it?

Using figure 2, Family Discipleship Time Plan, design what you'd like a typical month to look like for your family discipleship times. Think about not just when but also where, what, and who.

Example Family Discipleship Time Plan

	WEEK 1	WEEK 2
S	· Attend worship service together · Family Game/Movie Night	· Attend worship service together
M	· Bedtime: Read, Pray, Sing	· Bedtime: Read, Pray, Sing
T	· Bedtime: Read, Pray, Sing	· Bedtime: Read, Pray, Sing
W	· Bedtime: Read, Pray, Sing	· Meet with Home Group · Bedtime: Read, Pray, Sing
T	· Family devotional · Bedtime: Read, Pray, Sing	· Family devotional · Bedtime: Read, Pray, Sing
F	· Bedtime: Read, Pray, Sing	· Bedtime: Read, Pray, Sing
S	· Big Family Breakfast · One-on-one time with child	· Big Family Breakfast · Dinner with neighbors

Fig. 2

WEEK 3	WEEK 4	
· Attend worship service together	· Attend worship service together	S
· Bedtime: Read, Pray, Sing	· Bedtime: Read, Pray, Sing	M
· Bedtime: Read, Pray, Sing	· Bedtime: Read, Pray, Sing	T
· Meet with Home Group · Bedtime: Read, Pray, Sing	· Meet with Home Group · Bedtime: Read, Pray, Sing	W
· Family devotional · Bedtime: Read, Pray, Sing	· Family devotional · Bedtime: Read, Pray, Sing	T
· Bedtime: Read, Pray, Sing	· Bedtime: Read, Pray, Sing	F
· Big Family Breakfast	· Big Family Breakfast	S

Fig. 2 (continued)

Family Discipleship Time Plan

	WEEK 1	WEEK 2
S		
M		
T		
W		
T		
F		
S		

WEEK 3	WEEK 4	
		S
		M
		T
		W
		T
		F
		S

"We will not hide them from their children, / but tell to the coming generation / the glorious deeds of the LORD, and his might, / and the wonders that he has done." —Psalm 78:4

"As we sow we reap. Let us expect our children to know the Lord. Let us from the beginning mingle the name of Jesus with their ABC."[1] —Charles Spurgeon

"Though learning be found in schools, godliness is often received from the education of careful parents."[2] —Richard Baxter

"God gives to fallible parents this little boy or girl, who will certainly prove to be far from perfect, to love and train and teach, to bring up, in the "nurture and admonition", the training and instruction, of the Lord. It's a serious assignment. There is no higher calling."[3] —Elisabeth Elliot

"Masters of families, who preside in the other affairs of the house, must go before their households in the things of God . . . as such they must keep up family-doctrine, family-worship, and family-discipline: then is there a church in the house, and this is the family religion I am persuading you to."[4] —Matthew Henry

"The moment when I am most repelled by a child's behavior, that is my sign to *draw the very closest to that child*."[5] —Ann Voskamp

"Love is holy because it is like grace—the worthiness of its object is never really what matters."[6] —Marilynne Robinson

5

Moments

Family Discipleship Moments: Capturing and leveraging opportunities in the course of everyday life for the purpose of gospel-
centered conversations.

Every breath and every moment you get in this life is a sweet gift.
You've gotten a lot of them so far, though not one was promised to
you. Many of us take most of our parenting days for granted. Consider
that every moment you get with your kids is one less than you will
ever have again. Every minute you are together is a unique and special
opportunity you will never get back. Moments in time are precious
and they are nonrenewable, which is why we treasure them. We get
one shot for making the most of "right now," and while there may be
plenty of "try agains," there are no "do-overs." You cannot do today's
family discipleship tomorrow.

Family discipleship moments are about being prepared to take
advantage of opportunities to communicate God's truth in whatever
circumstances might come your way. Unlike family discipleship time,
moments do not happen through prearranged appointments. They are
less predictable but just as important. Since they are often impromptu,
an opportunity for a family discipleship moment could come at any

time. It could look like praying over a passing ambulance, stopping to smell and appreciate some flowers as part of God's good design, or pointing out someone's kind service to others as an example of what it looks like to follow Christ. You encounter myriad opportunities throughout your everyday life that you can use to communicate the goodness of God and what it looks like to follow him. There are great opportunities for discipleship in moments of discipline as well as moments of congratulations. A moment might be used to correct, to inform, or to encourage. Since your life can be unpredictable, we don't want you to be unprepared. The end of this chapter offers a long list of options and ideas for how you might use prepared language to your advantage in various situations as you leverage moments for the gospel.

Though we hope many family discipleship moments will lead to some deeper theological conversations, it usually doesn't take much to take advantage of a situation to communicate something true about God to your family. In a moment of disobedience, you remind your child of what God has commanded and the forgiveness he freely offers. When your family is facing difficulty and confusion, you declare that God is always in charge and your hope is set on him. Spontaneous, small, and simple conversations can remind your family of the truth of God without launching into a three-point sermon. You simply point out what God is doing and remind each other what God has done, a testament to how the gospel applies to every moment of your lives. You use your circumstances, as they unfold, to teach your family about the Lord and about themselves.

Your family has endless opportunities for family discipleship moments because, wherever you are, you are always in the presence of God. God is everywhere so family discipleship can happen anywhere. It often takes a high degree of readiness, vigilance, and a willingness to pause to take note of the evidence of God and applications of the gospel nearby. You will often fail to notice God even though he is all around you at all times. Even though he is intimately involved in all the insignificant details of your reality, even though "his invisible attributes, namely, his eternal power and divine nature, have been clearly perceived, ever since the creation of the world, in the things that have been made" (Rom. 1:20), even though you are his workmanship created in his image, you habitually overlook the presence of God. Your body that goes with you everywhere—your eyes and ears, your beating heart and breathing lungs, your intellect and imagination—can all declare his divinity. Testifying to God is not only appropriate everywhere, but also in every circumstance—in sunsets and storms, in celebration and sorrow, in the routine day as well as the extraordinary event. All of us are naturally skilled at ignoring and forgetting the constant work and closeness of God, so do what it takes to habitually be on the lookout for a good chance to bear witness. The almighty God is perpetually keeping you company. It does not require considerable effort to point out his presence, will, and work around you.

A discipleship moment can come and go in an instant, but don't let that make you underestimate its power. A single remark can change the trajectory of a person's life. In some ways this can be a little intimidating, but think of the awesome opportunity you have to be used as a gospel catalyst, a tiny spark of truth that ignites faith in your family. God can use one seemingly insignificant moment or ordinary conversation to create a cascading legacy, a chain reaction passing from generation to generation all started by planting a solitary seed of truth into your child's life today. Pray your child's heart will be good soil for the seeds of the gospel. Pray your kids will be the ones who hear the word and understand it. May they bear fruit and yield, and in some cases exponentially so, multiplying what they've received a hundred times over (Matt. 13:23). Pour your effort into planting and cultivating truth through your family's conversations. In other words, imagine how the Lord might use your seemingly small faithfulness in conversations today to bless your children as well as your children's children for a lifetime. Inside every single tiny redwood seed is the potential for a new forest of giants.

Not every moment has to be profound. Moments can be simple; you occasionally stop, look, listen, and encourage. This is how you pursue your children's hearts and not just address their behavior. This is how you can express genuine concern and love. First, stop everything else you are doing or are distracted by, and be fully present. Then look them in the eye. Listen to what they are feeling and not just what they are telling you, and encourage them with sincere words of genuine empathy and affirmation. It's not complicated, but it is deeply meaningful.

Since you cannot be sure when you will get the opportunity to speak life and love into your children, be committed to being available. When your children need a moment with you, you will want them to feel confident that your relationship with them makes you a safe person to approach as well as a safe person to be approached by. If they think every time you want to talk to them one-on-one it means they are in trouble, then they won't feel like they can initiate a conversation with you or feel secure hearing directly from you. Make it a habit to have regular one-on-one interaction built around encouragement and checking in. Find ways to use one-on-one moments to show that you care. If you want to be an effective disciple-maker, you have to be an effective relationship builder.

In Our Homes

Just like in your house, every kid in the Chandler home is different. What gets one excited makes another one roll his eyes. We are dealing with different souls that are bent in different ways, have different iniquities, and face different hurdles. Each one sees the world differently. There are thousands of variables and little moments that go into making each kid the way he or she is. Our hope is to take advantage of as many of those tiny moments for the gospel as we can.

I think the Chandlers are good at spontaneity and celebration and crediting God with what is good in life. But some of the most significant family discipleship moments for our family have come when my kids have come to me meekly or hurting and confessing sin, and I didn't freak out. I want my children to know they can safely come to me with hard things even if they think I will be disappointed. I want to extend grace whenever and wherever I can and in that teach them about the mercies and love of God. Forgiveness can make a potentially scary parent/child moment spiritually significant.

In the Griffin house we use many simple, repeatable, and memorable family discipleship phrases to leverage opportunities for gospel conversations. For example, with three young boys, we have a multitude of opportunities to address fighting. We have instilled in our boys that the only time it ever might be okay to push or punch is if it is necessary to protect someone. We teach them that God makes you strong to serve those who need strength. Our boys know it well enough now that all I need to do is ask, "When is the only time it is okay to push or punch?" When they respond, "To protect," we talk through whether that was the intention of their fighting.

More common than addressing aggression in our home is addressing fear. It is not uncommon for one of our young sons to have a nightmare or get spooked about something. We will often say to him individually or to all of them together, "Buddy, if God has got you, who can get you?" And they respond, "Nobody." Then I say, "And if God is for you, who can be against you?" And once again the answer is, "Nobody." Lastly I say, "And who can separate you from the love of God?" They say, "Nobody." And then I commend them for knowing these truths and remind them what they mean before we pray against succumbing to our irrational fears.

The Two Key Components of Moments

There are two key components to family discipleship moments. All of our spontaneous gospel interactions are attempts to communicate and teach these two things—the characteristics of God and godly character.

- *Characteristics of God.* To know God. (Who is God? What has he done? What is he doing? What is he like?)

- *Godly Character.* To grow in godliness. (Who am I? Who has God called me to be? What has he asked of me? How can I become more like him?)

Moments Teach the Characteristics of God

You have the divine task of teaching your kids who God is and what he is like. Taking advantage of spontaneous chances to either point out or verbalize your trust in who God is are prime educational opportunities. It is one thing to teach about God's faithfulness in an evening lecture around the dining room table. It is quite another to espouse that he will always do what he says he will in a moment when you are feeling forgotten or afraid and reading that "he will not leave you or forsake you" (Deut. 31:6), or that he will truly "give you rest" and that his "yoke is easy and [his] burden is light" (Matt. 11:28–30) in a moment when you are feeling overwhelmed by the weight of your responsibilities.

Your children's instincts and desires will often tell them to act in a way that departs from the path of God. Those are moments to remind them that God is wise, that he knows what is best. When your children are facing pronounced difficulty and can't understand "why God would let this happen," you will be ready to remind them that God is always in charge, that no one wrestled control away from God, that God is always good, and that their circumstances are not cruelty from God nor are they beyond his reach to intervene. When your child struggles with prayer, you'll be quick to emphasize that God wants to talk with us. These heartfelt and profound truths sprinkled throughout your family's interactions are a simple yet significant part of leading your family spiritually.

It is a great comfort to a child to know who God is and what he is like. If the goal of our discipleship is trust in Christ, then any moment we can use to tell them about Jesus and his trustworthiness is a step in the right direction. Remind your children of what God has done in the past and what you see him doing in their lives now as well as what you hope he'll do in the future. God is a personal God, and you have the chance to continually reintroduce your family to him while praising him for who he is and what he's done.

The ultimate example of what God has done for your family is found in the life, death, and resurrection of Jesus Christ. A thorough and clear understanding of the gospel will greatly benefit your family discipleship moments. It will bless your kids to know that everyone needs Jesus, that Jesus came to save sinners, and that he is merciful; God does not give his children the punishment they deserve. Lead with a gospel perspective that reminds your family of the grace and forgiveness of Christ as well as our daily battle to joyfully walk in obedience to our loving heavenly Father. Teach them all the praiseworthy attributes of God, because you desire to see them praising God with their whole being.

Moments Teach Godly Character

Your job is to "train up a child in the way he should go" (Prov. 22:6). This requires frequent course setting and course correction. Your children's character will tell you a lot about where their heart is with the Lord. "Even a child makes himself known by his acts, / by whether his conduct is pure and upright" (Prov. 20:11). Being both an encourager who fans into flame the godly characteristics you want to see and a disciplinarian who addresses the missteps is essential work for you as a Christian parent. You will find your family both forgiving and affirming one another as saints—sometimes in the same moment.

Family discipleship moments are prime opportunities to point out ways to walk in godly character. One of the best ways to disciple your kids in godly character is to seek ways to encourage your children when they demonstrate various fruits of the Spirit. Look for a chance to spontaneously point out and celebrate your child's joy, delighting in things that honor God. When things get difficult, say a quick prayer together for peace, a calm confidence in God's goodness and power. You'll never run out of chances to talk about patience, being slow to anger, waiting kindly and quietly.

Of course, everyone's character is flawed. That is why it is essential that you address sin in your child's life through gospel-centered family discipleship moments. You will frequently be presented with opportunities to teach your kids about both the seriousness of sin and God's generosity with grace. You want to encourage freedom from obedience to our sinful thoughts and emotions, and to call your children to walk in grace-driven integrity. But because we all sin, we must have regular moments of repentance. You will foster merciful and loving conversations for your children to confess their sin and turn away from it to follow Jesus as you extend forgiveness, releasing them from their wrong. You will also lovingly institute appropriate consequences as well as point them back toward holiness and accountability. You will remind them often that God's love does not ebb and flow with their behavior, and neither does yours, but because he loves his people he has called them to a better way to live. This will be a well-practiced routine in any Christian household.

Leveraging moments to disciple your children will often involve the direct use of God's word applied to your situation. "For the word of God is living and active, sharper than any two-edged sword, piercing to the division of soul and of spirit, of joints and of marrow, and discerning the thoughts and intentions of the heart" (Heb. 4:12). You will find a list of ways to use Scripture in family discipleship moments at the end of this chapter. It is important here to acknowledge the common and often subtle temptation to abuse the Bible to suit your own needs and desires in behavior modification. It is easy to slip into a habit of applying what God has said in order to manipulate circumstances so you can get what you want. Family discipleship is not about using Scripture as a means to get your own way. A disciple is not a marionette, a bridled child whose strings you pull when and where you wish. Your child is an apprentice invited to learn and practice under the loving guidance of a caretaker. Parenting is about godly concern for the benefit of children in the name of Christ, not worldly coercion for your own selfish sake.

We use God's word because it is perfect. It will never pass away so it will be there for your child long after you are not. Scripture is a gift of wisdom from the Lord, something children are in desperate daily need of. Remember, much of family discipleship is modeling. In every situation your kids will be looking to you to be the living example of God's truth—that includes how you use God's word.

Jesus Discipled in Moments

Jesus frequently captured and leveraged discipleship moments. His lessons often involved pointing out something theological about the situation he and his disciples found themselves in. Here are three examples from Luke of Jesus demonstrating situational discipleship.

In Luke 21:1–4, Christ pointed out to his disciples a widow who dropped two copper coins into the offering box. Christ uses this opportunity to teach his disciples about kingdom economics. Though she didn't give as large an amount as the wealthy, she gave all she had to the offering box out of heartfelt devotion to God. Heart devotion is what God wants, not lavish offerings to impress our neighbors. In Luke 13:1–5, a group of people ask Jesus about a recent event in order to get his theological perspective. He uses another current event, a tower falling on some people, to call everyone to repentance and away from superstition about why bad things happen. In Luke 11:37–12:3, Christ takes advantage of an opportunity to confront sin where and when he sees it, something every parent needs to be ready to do with Christlike exactitude and gentleness. In Luke 18:18–27, Jesus responds to a rich young ruler's questions by encouraging him to sell all he has. He uses the moment to turn to his disciples and teach them about how God can overcome all of our impediments to faith, including our earthly wealth and security.

Jesus also regularly demonstrated the usefulness of knowing Scripture in addressing theological questions and guiding those who need guidance. In admonishing the Pharisees about creating their own laws instead of following God's, Jesus quotes the fifth commandment and points out where they've strayed from what God intended in his word. "God commanded, 'Honor your father and your mother,' and,

'Whoever reviles father or mother must surely die.' But you say, 'If any-one tells his father or his mother, "What you would have gained from me is given to God," he need not honor his father.' So for the sake of your tradition you have made void the word of God" (Matt. 15:4–6). The Bible contains many more examples of Jesus teaching his follow-ers about God and how to be godly by using both the circumstances around him and Scripture as he did so. You, likewise, can lean on the word of God in conversations as you lead your family.

Developing Family Discipleship Language

A great way to be prepared for family discipleship moments in your household is to have a unified, precrafted language. Deciding on family language, values, and goals with your spouse or close community will help you to be on the same page when opportunities arise, and it will assist in maintaining a level of consistency, regardless of who is having the conversation with your children.

We've provided some language that may assist you in capturing your family discipleship moments. You might consider implementing the list below in conversations in your home as you talk about God and what it means to be godly. These short phrases can be used to answer many of life's questions and can be applied to a multitude of circumstances. Imagine getting on your children's level, looking them in the eyes, and speaking these truths in a loving manner. Circle or underline the words or Scriptures that you would like to start con-sistently using in your home as you recognize and capture family discipleship moments.

Five Foundational Truths

The Village Church NextGen ministry holds to the following founda-tional truths:
1. Jesus came to save sinners.
2. God is good.
3. God is in charge of everything.

4. God wants to talk with us.

5. God made everything.

Ten Foundational Truths

Similar to TVC's Five Foundational Truths, Eastside Community Church uses these Ten Foundational Truths consistently across its statement of faith, adult teaching ministry, and kid's ministry:

1. God's word is true.

2. God is triune.

3. God is always good.

4. God is always in charge.

5. God made everyone and everything.

6. God loves people.

7. Everyone needs Jesus.

8. Jesus saves his people.

9. God hears his people.

10. God's people follow Jesus.

Characteristics or Attributes of God

1. *Wise.* God knows what is best.

2. *Generous.* God gives what is best.

3. *Loving.* God does what is best.

4. *Good.* God is what is best.

5. *Unchanging.* God was, is, and always will be the same.

6. *Creator.* God made everyone and everything.

7. *Just.* God is right to punish sin.

8. *Faithful.* God always does what he says he will do.

9. *Provider.* God meets the needs of his children.

10. *Merciful.* God does not give his children the punishment they deserve.

11. *Attentive.* God hears and responds to the prayers of his children.

12. *Almighty.* Nothing is too hard for God.

13. *Compassionate.* God sees, cares, and acts when his children are in need.

14. *Worthy.* Only God deserves all glory.
15. *Deliverer.* God rescues his children.

Godly Character

1. *Patience.* Being slow to anger, waiting kindly and quietly.
2. *Joy.* Delighting in things that honor God.
3. *Peace.* A calm confidence in God's goodness and power.
4. *Love.* A caring commitment to God and others over yourself.
5. *Goodness.* Doing the right thing, at the right time, for the right reason.
6. *Kindness.* Being generous with your possessions, your words, and your actions.
7. *Gentleness.* Expressing compassion in words and actions.
8. *Self-Control.* Freedom from obedience to our sinful thoughts and emotions.

Christian Vocabulary and Phrases

1. *Repentance.* To confess your sin and turn away from it to follow Jesus.
2. *Glorify.* To show, honor, and enjoy God as most valuable.
3. *Pride.* To show, honor, and enjoy yourself as most valuable.
4. *Authority.* The right to be in charge.
5. *Compassion.* To see, care, and act when others are in need.
6. *Worship.* The right response to the goodness of God.
7. *Daily bread.* Everything we need to gladly glorify the Father.
8. *Forgiveness.* To release someone from their wrong.
9. *Disciple.* A friend and follower of Jesus.
10. *Confession.* Telling the truth about your sin.
11. *Grace.* God freely gives his children what they don't deserve.
12. *Gospel.* The good news of God's plan to rescue the world from the problem of sin through Jesus Christ.
13. *God's children.* Those who love and trust Jesus.
14. *God adopts* into his family those who love and trust Jesus.
15. *The kingdom of heaven.* Where Jesus is honored as the highest and best King.

16. *Heaven* is good because God is there.
17. *The Bible.* God's true word. It is from God and about God.
18. *Jesus.* When we look at Jesus, we see what God is like (because Jesus is God).
19. *Prayer.* We pray to the Father because of the Son with the help of the Holy Spirit. Here are five types of prayer:

- *Praise and adoration:* Telling God how great he is.
- *Thanksgiving:* Thanking God for what he does and gives.
- *Confession.* Telling the truth about your sin.
- *Request.* Asking God to do or give something.
- *Intercession.* Asking God for something on someone else's behalf.

20. There are two ways we can know what is true. We can know with our minds: *understanding.* We can know with our hearts: *belief.*
21. *Sin.* It's more than just the bad things we think, feel, do, and say; it's why we do them. Our hearts are sick with sin.
22. *Sinful nature.* All people are slaves of sin; we both choose to sin and have no choice but to sin.
23. *Forgiveness.* God forgives fully, freely, and forever.

- *Fully:* All of your sin is forgiven, and it is forgiven in full. All my sin, all the way.
- *Freely:* Forgiveness is a gift, not something you can earn or deserve.
- *Forever:* God's forgiveness is lasting. He does not change his mind or take back his forgiveness.

Examples in Scripture

You might consider using the following scriptures in various circumstances as you capture moments in the life of your household for the sake of the gospel.

"One Another" Verses

Many scriptures speak about how we interact with one another. These can be very useful in family discipleship moments.

- "Just as [Jesus has] loved you, you also are to love one another" (John 13:34).
- "Outdo one another in showing honor" (Rom. 12:10).
- "Therefore welcome one another as Christ has welcomed you, for the glory of God" (Rom. 15:7).
- "For you were called to freedom. . . . Only do not use your freedom as an opportunity for the flesh, but through love serve one another" (Gal. 5:13).
- "Let us not become conceited, provoking one another, envying one another" (Gal. 5:26).
- "If anyone is caught in any transgression, you who are spiritual should restore him in a spirit of gentleness. Keep watch on yourself, lest you too be tempted" (Gal. 6:1).
- "Be kind to one another, tenderhearted, forgiving one another, as God in Christ forgave you" (Eph. 4:32).
- "Do not lie to one another, seeing that you have put off the old self with its practices" (Col. 3:9).
- "Therefore encourage one another and build one another up" (1 Thess. 5:11).
- "See that no one repays anyone evil for evil, but always seek to do good to one another and to everyone" (1 Thess. 5:15).
- "And let us consider how to stir up one another to love and good works" (Heb. 10:24).
- "Do not speak evil against one another" (James 4:11).
- "Show hospitality to one another without grumbling" (1 Pet. 4:9).
- "Beloved, let us love one another, for love is from God, and whoever loves has been born of God and knows God" (1 John 4:7).

Diligence/Work Ethic

- "And let us not grow weary of doing good, for in due season we will reap, if we do not give up" (Gal. 6:9).
- "Whatever you do, work heartily, as for the Lord and not for men, knowing that from the Lord you will receive the inheritance as your reward. You are serving the Lord Christ" (Col. 3:23–24).

Sadness

- "My soul melts away for sorrow; / strengthen me according to your word!" (Ps. 119:28).
- "Come to me, all who labor and are heavy laden, and I will give you rest" (Matt. 11:28).
- "He will wipe away every tear from their eyes, and death shall be no more, neither shall there be mourning, nor crying, nor pain anymore, for the former things have passed away" (Rev. 21:4).

Gladness

- "But the righteous shall be glad; / they shall exult before God; / they shall be jubilant with joy!" (Ps. 68:3).
- "Nevertheless, do not rejoice in this, that the spirits are subject to you, but rejoice that your names are written in heaven" (Luke 10:20).

Anger

- "Refrain from anger, and forsake wrath! / Fret not yourself; it tends only to evil" (Ps. 37:8).
- "Be angry and do not sin; do not let the sun go down on your anger, and give no opportunity to the devil" (Eph. 4:26–27).

Complaining

- "Do all things without grumbling or disputing, that you may be blameless and innocent, children of God without blemish in the midst of a crooked and twisted generation, among whom you shine as lights in the world" (Phil. 2:14–15).

Fear/Courage

- "Have I not commanded you? Be strong and courageous. Do not be frightened, and do not be dismayed, for the LORD your God is with you wherever you go" (Josh. 1:9).
- "When I am afraid, / I put my trust in you" (Ps. 56:3).
- "Blessed is the man who trusts in the LORD, whose trust is the LORD" (Jer. 17:7).
- "So we can confidently say, 'The Lord is my helper; / I will not fear; / what can man do to me?'" (Heb. 13:6).

Encouragement

- "But exhort one another every day, as long as it is called 'today,' that none of you may be hardened by the deceitfulness of sin" (Heb. 3:13).

Forgiveness

- "Pay attention to yourselves! If your brother sins, rebuke him, and if he repents, forgive him" (Luke 17:3).
- "If we confess our sins, he is faithful and just to forgive us our sins and to cleanse us from all unrighteousness" (1 John 1:9).

Humility/Servanthood

- "Do nothing from selfish ambition or conceit, but in humility count others more significant than yourselves" (Phil. 2:3).
- "Whoever serves, as one who serves by the strength that God supplies—in order that in everything God may be glorified through Jesus Christ" (1 Pet. 4:11).

Hardship/Suffering

- "The LORD is good, / a stronghold in the day of trouble; / he knows those who take refuge in him" (Nah. 1:7).
- "I have said these things to you, that in me you may have peace. In the world you will have tribulation. But take heart; I have overcome the world" (John 16:33).

- "So we do not lose heart. Though our outer self is wasting away, our inner self is being renewed day by day" (2 Cor. 4:16).

Anxiety/Insecurity

- "I have set the LORD always before me; / because he is at my right hand, I shall not be shaken. Therefore my heart is glad, and my whole being rejoices; / my flesh also dwells secure" (Ps. 16:8–9).
- "Fear not, for I am with you; / be not dismayed, for I am your God; / I will strengthen you, I will help you, / I will uphold you with my righteous right hand" (Isa. 41:10).
- "But seek first the kingdom of God and his righteousness, and all these things will be added to you. Therefore do not be anxious about tomorrow, for tomorrow will be anxious for itself. Sufficient for the day is its own trouble" (Matt. 6:33–34).
- "Humble yourselves, therefore, under the mighty hand of God so that at the proper time he may exalt you, casting all your anxieties on him, because he cares for you" (1 Pet. 5:6–7).

Honesty/Integrity

- "Whoever walks in integrity walks securely, / but he who makes his ways crooked will be found out" (Prov. 10:9).
- "Lying lips are an abomination to the LORD, / but those who act faithfully are his delight" (Prov. 12:22).
- "Let your 'yes' be yes and your 'no' be no, so that you may not fall under condemnation" (James 5:12).

Kindness

- "And as you wish that others would do to you, do so to them" (Luke 6:31).
- "See that no one repays anyone evil for evil, but always seek to do good to one another and to everyone" (1 Thess. 5:15).

Temptation

- "Finally, be strong in the Lord and in the strength of his might. Put on the whole armor of God, that you may be able to stand against the schemes of the devil" (Eph. 6:10–11).
- "Be sober-minded; be watchful. Your adversary the devil prowls around like a roaring lion, seeking someone to devour. Resist him, firm in your faith" (1 Pet. 5:8–9).

Identity

- "But to all who did receive him, who believed in his name, he gave the right to become children of God" (John 1:12).
- "Therefore, if anyone is in Christ, he is a new creation. The old has passed away; behold, the new has come" (2 Cor. 5:17).
- "I have been crucified with Christ. It is no longer I who live, but Christ who lives in me. And the life I now live in the flesh I live by faith in the Son of God, who loved me and gave himself for me" (Gal. 2:20).
- "He predestined us for adoption as sons to himself through Jesus Christ, according to the purpose of his will" (Eph. 1:5).

The Ten Commandments (Ex. 20:3–17)

- "You shall have no other gods before me."
- "You shall not make for yourself a carved image, or any likeness of anything that is in heaven above, or that is in the earth beneath, or that is in the water under the earth."
- "You shall not take the name of the LORD your God in vain."
- "Remember the Sabbath day, to keep it holy."
- "Honor your father and your mother, that your days may be long in the land that the LORD your God is giving you."
- "You shall not murder."
- "You shall not commit adultery."
- "You shall not steal."

- "You shall not bear false witness against your neighbor."
- "You shall not covet your neighbor's house; you shall not covet your neighbor's wife, or his male servant, or his female servant, or his ox, or his donkey, or anything that is your neighbor's."

Conclusion

Family discipleship moments are capturing and leveraging opportunities in the course of everyday life for the purpose of gospel-centered conversations. As a parent, seeking to disciple as Jesus discipled means being attentive and alert, looking for opportunities to train your children by applying biblical truth to your present circumstances. Memorizing God's word can make you a more effective disciple-maker and help you leverage family discipleship moments for the sake of gospel conversation.

Questions

1. Can you think of an unplanned event or conversation that has had a profound impact on your life? What was it?

2. Make a list of the goals you have in the discipleship of your family. Think about what you want your children to know and what you want to see formed in them.

3. How are your everyday interactions with each other working toward those goals? If they aren't currently, how can they?

4. Can you think of a time you had an unplanned conversation about spiritual matters with your family? How did it go? What could have made it better?

5. What is your practice of confession and repentance like in your home? Making a mistake and asking forgiveness can be a great family discipleship moment for parents as well as kids. How can your family grow in the way you practice repentance?

6. Are there pervasive idols or ungodly habits in the life of your household that could be addressed with kind words in a family discipleship moment?

7. If you have more than one child, how are your children different? How does that impact what you are trying to do in discipling each of them?

Read through the language examples on pages 122–31 again, and then consider the following questions.

8. What are the attributes of God you'd like your kids to be well aware of? What kinds of circumstances might you be able to leverage to communicate those attributes? What will you say?

9. What are character traits and fruits of the Spirit you'd like to see your kids exemplify? What common situations might be opportunities to foster those traits? What will you say?

10. What words or phrases stuck out to you as you read through the list? How might you use them in speaking to your family?

11. What will you say to create a family discipleship moment in the following circumstances (think about scriptures you might use as well as phrases you might apply consistently):

   a. When your child is angry.

   b. When your child is sad.

   c. When you have something to celebrate.

   d. When you see something upsetting.

   e. When your child is scared.

   f. When you messed up and want to apologize.

g. When you see something beautiful.

h. When you see sinful pride in your child.

i. When your kids are having trouble getting along.

j. When your child overcomes a fear.

"And he said to the people of Israel, 'When your children ask their fathers in times to come, "What do these stones mean?" then you shall let your children know, "Israel passed over this Jordan on dry ground." For the LORD your God dried up the waters of the Jordan for you until you passed over, as the LORD your God did to the Red Sea, which he dried up for us until we passed over, so that all the peoples of the earth may know that the hand of the LORD is mighty, that you may fear the LORD your God forever.'" —Joshua 4:21–24

"Would that parents would awaken to a sense of the importance of this matter. It is a pleasant duty to talk of Jesus to our sons and daughters, and the more so because it has often proved to be an accepted work, for God has saved the children through the parents' prayers and admonitions."[1] —Charles Spurgeon

"My mother, Thy faithful one, weeping to Thee for me, more than mothers weep the bodily deaths of their children. For she, by that faith and spirit which she had from Thee, discerned the death wherein I lay, and Thou heardest her, O Lord; Thou heardest her, and despisedst not her tears, when streaming down, they watered the ground under her eyes in every place where she prayed. . . . For almost nine years passed, in which I wallowed in the mire of that deep pit, and the darkness of falsehood, often assaying to rise, but dashed down the more grievously. All which time that chaste, godly and sober widow (such as Thou lovest), now more cheered with hope, yet no while relaxing in her weeping and mourning, ceased not at all hours of her devotions to bewail my case unto Thee. And her prayers entered into Thy presence."[2] —St. Augustine of Hippo

"I remember [my mother's] prayers . . . and they have always followed me. They have clung to me all my life."[3] —Abraham Lincoln

"The greatest legacy one can pass on to one's children and grandchildren is not money or other material things accumulated in one's life, but rather a legacy of character and faith."[4] —Billy Graham

6

Milestones

Family Discipleship Milestones: Marking and making occasions to celebrate and commemorate significant spiritual milestones of God's work in the life of the family and child.

Seeds and stones can both produce natural concentric circles—rings and ripples. A stone tossed into a pond makes ripples, small waves flowing from the center. In a like manner, an acorn planted in the ground makes tree rings, circular lines inside the trunk that mark a winter that has passed. The stone's impact is quick and clear until it sinks below the surface, and then its effects quickly dissipate and disappear. Inversely, an acorn's impact is invisible at first, spreads much, much slower, and lasts much, much longer. It even reproduces its effects as it matures and multiplies. Much of your family discipleship will feel like stones in a pond—making a quick impact but lacking clear lasting effects. Some of it, however, may have an imperceivable influence at first, but will slowly grow into something deeply rooted and multiplying. Some aspects of your family discipleship will be meaningful and memorable for a lifetime and will continue to produce fruit in generations to come. Some of the most meaningful, lasting, and unforgettable aspects of your household discipleship will be accomplished in cele-brating and commemorating spiritual milestones.

Milestones are, in some ways, a more significant version of family discipleship time and family discipleship moments. Though watched for, sometimes milestones will happen unpredictably. Other times, they will be well orchestrated and planned by you. Though time and mo-ments can result in fantastic accumulated discipleship, sometimes as individual instances they can be forgotten. But milestones are those points in time that stick with you and your kids, and they offer you the chance to take special note of what God is doing in and through your family. Milestones make lasting memories together as a family of God and create things that help us remember so we won't forget.

In our culture we celebrate many milestones. We celebrate mile-stones of age in birthdays, of marriage in anniversaries, and of accom-plishments with awards, licenses, or degrees. Ceremonies, rituals, and traditions around milestones are all common. If you imagine your life like a line graph of events, milestones are likely both the highest peaks and the lowest valleys. God has wired us to be people who remember, and it's the extraordinary events that really stay with us.

A family discipleship milestone is an event or change that is so important or profound that it is worthy of recurring reflection. It could be something that brings joy upon remembering, like the birth or adoption of a child, or something that brings up difficulty or pain, like the loss of a loved one. What all family discipleship milestones have in common is that they are all experiences that bear witness to God's faithfulness.

Of course, milestones are not the only times that a family should be discipling, but they should be a large part of an overall plan to see your kids brought up in the Lord. Family discipleship milestones are also a tremendous opportunity to extend the discipleship process to your child's extended family, friends, neighbors, and biblical community. Significant occasions are opportunities to share about what the Lord has done and what he is doing.

The goal of a milestone is, in large part, remembrance—that you would not forget God's rightful place in your life and all that he is doing in and through you. It would seem wise, therefore, to commend you to decide as a family where you could record what the Lord has done. Write down memories and milestones as a family and save that record so you can access it later. Use a journal, a photo album, or a special repository for notes. Never underestimate the power of a handwritten letter to your children. Your words and thoughts etched into permanence by putting them on paper is an instant heirloom. God's people have often used something physical to remind them of something spiritual.

In 1 Samuel 7:12, Samuel places a large stone in a field. He names the stone Ebenezer, which means "stone of help." This stone was a memorial of a battle that the Lord won for his people. Unfortunately, less than a generation later the people were asking for a king who would "go out before us and fight our battles" (1 Sam. 8:20). Even with a monument, they forgot. Good family discipleship milestones won't just be one-off events or objects, but something that will follow your children throughout their lives so that they will not forget the faithfulness of God. What is your family's Ebenezer? How will you keep from forgetting?

In Our Homes

In the Chandler house, we have had plenty to celebrate, but some of the most significant family discipleship milestones and spiritual celebrations have also centered around some of our darkest experiences. Ever since I was diagnosed with cancer, "scan day" has become one of the biggest spiritually significant events of our year. Every time I get a scan to see if cancer has returned to my brain, it is an occasion to commemorate that God is faithful, that he is good, and that he healed and preserved my kids' daddy. We make a big deal out of "scan day."

We have also worked hard to create some meaningful family discipleship milestones for my kids centered on their spiritual development and maturity. When a Chandler child turns thirteen, we throw a rite-of-passage birthday party. We have a big celebration with friends, we feast, and we use the opportunity to usher the child into adulthood.

We invite other spiritually influential adults to join their grandparents, mom, and me in calling out virtues that we see in our child. The adults write and read letters describing the godly traits that they have witnessed in the life of my son or daughter. We acknowledge who they are and not just what they do. We encourage them to grow in those attributes that are admirable, and I give some words of warning about what this next season of life may look like. At my son's thirteenth birthday, this ceremony also came with some heirlooms of remembrance. I gave him a knife with a deer antler grip, and one of the other men gave him a hammer—not his grandfather's hammer, or his father's hammer, but his own hammer to help remind him that the life of manhood that he is now starting is his own. These mementos serve as reminders of the words spoken and mark the life change that comes with the move into adulthood.

In the Griffin home, the first gift we ever gave our sons was on the day of their birth, and we hope it is something worth reflecting on for a lifetime—the gift of their names. Each of our sons was given a biblical middle name whose meaning was an attribute of God. For Oscar it is Samuel—God hears. For Gus it is Joshua—God saves. For Theodore it is Jude—God is worthy of praise. Many of the things we give our kids will come and go, but their names are uniquely theirs and will be an ever-present reminder of who their family's God is and what he does. This, like many forms of family discipleship, happens before they are even aware.

One part of the Griffin family milestone plan has become a near daily discipline for me. I am making a considerable personal investment in a Journal Bible for each of my young boys. For each individual son, I am reading and writing my way through a leather Journal Bible (a Bible with wide margins built for extensive notes). As I read, I write little notes of insight about the text, personal encouragements, and prayers for that son. One day I will give each son his completed personally annotated Bible as an heirloom of my love for him and my desire to see each one carry on our family legacy of walking with the Lord. Though we have not planned exactly when we will give the journals to them, be it at baptism or an important birthday, the plan is that it will be incorporated into a Griffin rite of passage. It's a gift that I hope keeps on giving.

The Two Kinds of Milestones

There are two kinds of family discipleship milestones. Some milestones we make, and some milestones we mark.

- *Making.* Creating significant milestones to commemorate, celebrate, or commend spiritual growth.
- *Marking.* Appreciating God and his unpredictable work as you recognize it in your family.

Making or Marking

Many of the best family discipleship milestones will be manufactured by you (made). You can make a milestone out of a variety of opportunities. Memorable "firsts" can be great options—first Bible, first paycheck, first Communion, and so on. Take advantage of those "firsts" to point out the attributes of God, and attach God's faithfulness to the memories of those new beginnings. Instead of just giving something to a child—a diploma, car keys, an heirloom, a responsibility—make the presentation of that item a ritual with some pomp and circumstance. Adding some fanfare to a moment helps create a memory and communicate the weight of what's happening. Find ways to display your heart and God's will for your child by injecting some creativity and formality into significant moments in your child's life. Feast, toast, pray, lay hands, give a speech, write a poem, share, sing, reward, and document in ways that fully announce and record the magnitude of the milestone.

Milestones do not have to be new events on your family calendar. You can find simple ways to make events that are already happening spiritually memorable. On an annual family vacation you can include time to spiritually grow together through worship, prayer, and reflecting on all the Lord has done in the past year. Start a wedding anniversary tradition of reflecting as a family on God's faithfulness in your marriage. It's not hard to leverage holidays to be spiritual milestone rituals—focusing on gratitude at Thanksgiving, on anticipation and need at Advent, on generosity at Christmas, on resolutions for change at New Year's, on sacrifice and suffering at Lent, and on the gospel of God's victory over sin and death at Easter.

You could also consider how you can honor individuals in your family and commend them to the Lord on more individualized holidays. Read Proverbs 31:10–31 and pray over the moms in your family on Mother's Day. Read Psalm 112 and pray over the dads in your family on Father's Day. Make praying specific blessings over family members part of your birthday traditions at each family member's birthday. All of these are opportunities to point to God's faithfulness in days that you are probably already celebrating.

Some of your family discipleship milestones will happen less predictably. When they happen, even unexpectedly, you'll be able to take the time to appreciate and recognize what God has done. These are milestones for you to mark. Unlike *making* family discipleship milestones, *marking* is what we do to commemorate the work of God in our children's lives in ways that we did not see coming. You can make a milestone out of an important birthday or out of high school graduation because you know when they will happen. However, for unforeseen big life events, like when your son or daughter becomes a Christian or when a loved one dies or when someone receives a devastating diagnosis, you can find ways to mark and commemorate what God has done even though you didn't know when or if it would happen.

When someone in your family becomes a Christian, Christ himself gave us a milestone ritual to perform together—baptism. There may be no sweeter moment in the life of your family than marking someone's salvation by baptizing him or her in the name of the Father, Son, and Holy Spirit. This God-instituted ritual reminds us that who we used to be is buried with Christ and we have risen to newness of life in the truth of the gospel. Make baptism as big a celebration as you can. We know that in heaven "there is joy before the angels of God over one sinner who repents" (Luke 15:10). Couple a baptism with a feast, a memento, a toast, or anything else you can think of to commemorate that your family member "has passed from death to life" (John 5:24).

Milestones are not always celebratory. How you mark the darkest and most difficult milestones will have a profound impact on your family. Think about how break-ups, divorce, abusive incidents, disease, and death can mark a person's life. You are the guardian of these young souls, and they will look to you to tell them truths that serve as a firm foundation when the storms of life assail them. You'll remind them that in the "valley of the shadow of death" they need fear no evil, for God is still with them (Ps. 23:4). That God is the "God of all comfort" (2 Cor. 1:3). That God is "near to the brokenhearted" (Ps. 34:18). That your family trusts God like a tree that is planted by water so you do not get anxious about whether there is a downpour or drought (Jer. 17:7–8).

The death of a loved one, in particular, can be a significant milestone for your son or daughter. A funeral is a profound event in anyone's life, but it's especially so for a child. It's a time of talking about loving memories, sorrow, and mortality. Eternal life is a sweet comfort to believing families in moments of loss, but that does not make that time free of grief or pain. Some of the most meaningful collective memories for your family may be around the hardest days you've faced together. Going forward, you might create a tradition of visiting the graves of loved ones you've lost on the anniversary of their passing. Flowers, phone calls, and letters are great ways to commemorate loss and let each other know you have not forgotten. Leverage those dark times to remind each other of all you have in Christ, who conquered death.

Passing on Your Faith through Milestones

Your faith is your children's best possible inheritance. Pass it on to them as often and thoroughly as you can. Since faith grows, expands, and multiplies, there will always be enough for every one of your potential descendants. There are many ways you can make milestones special opportunities to pass on your faith. Here is a short list of examples for you to consider as you approach making your milestone plan at the end of this chapter.

Heirlooms and mementos. Consider what physical items you might give to your children as a symbol of their Christian heritage. This is not commodifying your legacy; this is reminding them of their part in Christ's. This could be a family keepsake, a cross necklace, a purity ring, a new Bible, a letter, a pocketknife, a tool, or their first (fill-in-the-blank). Maybe you have something that was handed down to you that you can hand down to them in order to remind them of the family tradition of faithfulness to your God. Giving a gift may also serve as a symbol of a day worth remembering. Connect the gift with an important event so that they will see it and associate it with what the Lord has done. Similar to the way a bride and groom exchange rings on their wedding day to remind one another of their vows, you can give your children objects that will remind them of the covenant relationship they have with God.

Rituals and traditions. Decorating a Christmas tree, singing "Happy Birthday," hunting for Easter eggs—these are all common family traditions. Creating annual traditions infused with gospel truth is a great way to hand down your faith to your children. Traditions are a customary practice that you pass on to your kids by habitually acting them out together. Similarly, rituals are the established way you practice your religion collectively. Traditions and rituals are an important aspect of milestones since they happen repeatedly and repetition leads both to learning and to remembrance. Find ways to create and foster new family traditions that communicate your faith in the God of the Bible.

A rite of passage is a significant ritual that communicates the shift from childhood to adulthood. We described what this looks like in the Chandler house earlier in this chapter. Rituals are powerful opportunities because they go beyond the normal rhythm of your family into something momentous. Some churches have ceremonies like this built into their rhythms, like the rite of confirmation or a purity ceremony. We highly recommend making a rite-of-passage ceremony a part of your milestone plan.

Events and experiences. Creating an experience can take an ordinary event in a person's life and elevate it to something extraordinary. Think about all the engagement stories you have ever heard. Most of them do not involve the simple gift of a ring. There is something about the elaborate nature of the surprise that communicates genuine love and thoughtfulness. The more the man uniquely caters the fanfare to the bride, the more she appreciates his effort and the more clearly his affection is communicated. Think of your children's family discipleship milestones in the same way. How can you turn a time of recognizing or celebrating what the Lord has done into an event or an experience they will never forget? Would they love to find the keys to their first car at the end of a scavenger hunt you designed? Would they appreciate going out to lunch at their favorite restaurant and receiving a cross necklace after their first time taking Communion? Would they be delighted by a letter or toast from you about your parental pride, heartfelt prayers, and trust as you allow them to start dating? How can you make their first school dance, church retreat, graduation, wedding, mission trip, or first day at a new job a spiritually influential event?

Crafts and projects. If you are crafty or handy, consider how making or building something together could be part of a milestone for your child. Finishing a functional or artistic project can be a great memory-forming activity for your family. Your finished product is a testament to time spent together and the lessons and messages learned along the way.

Feasts and fasts. Both feasting and fasting are great ways to commemorate the Lord's work. Feasting celebrates the Lord's grace and generosity toward you. Traditionally fasting for a season can help your family remember that God is all they need. You can mark what God is doing through abundance or with deprivation, as long as the focus is on your praiseworthy God.

Monuments and memorials. In Scripture the people of God often erected monuments to remind them of all the Lord had done. If an heirloom is a memento that can go with you anywhere, a monument is more like something built and left in a place that is significant, similar to the way we use a gravestone as a memorial of someone's life. A tree planted at a family home, a family name carved in the wet cement of a sidewalk, a special brick or cornerstone laid into the wall of a new house, a word or phrase carved into the trunk of a tree—these are all examples of physical monuments that can be used in teaching your children something about God in ways they can literally look back at and remember. You might want to make a family time capsule. Fill something with precious letters or mementos and open it one day on a memorable date for your family.

Responsibility and authority. After your children reach a milestone spiritually or physically, you might consider how to give them new responsibilities. This could be coming to the main worship service with mom and dad, getting a driver's license, getting a job, taking Communion, reaching a savings goal, cooking for themselves, doing laundry or yard work, paying a family bill, serving in ministry, and so on. Responsibilities communicate trust and teach accountability. Handing off responsibility to your children can be a great way to entrust them with authority.

Symbols and crests. Christianity is a faith bursting with symbols, including the ichthus, the dove, the alpha and omega, the Trinity knot, and, of course, the cross. Symbols are packed with meaning and memory, and so they make powerful additions to family discipleship milestones. For hundreds of years, some families have incorporated a family crest, something like a trademark symbol for their family. Creating or implementing a symbol unique to your family can be a creative way of crystalizing your family's legacy and priorities.

Journeys and destinations. A pilgrimage is a journey with a religious purpose. Touring the geography of the Bible in Israel is a fantastic pilgrimage, but you don't have to go far from home to take an important family trip. Journeys make great family discipleship milestones as they are adventures fraught with teachable moments and predisposed to making life-long memories. The journey can make the destination special; how you get there is as important as where you are going. Take a train, boat, bike, or a simple road trip for travel's sake, and make the journey special. You know what would truly delight your family and be spiritually significant so use what you know about your children to creatively design a milestone journey. You might plan a wilderness adventure full of camping, canoeing, fishing, hunting, and hiking. Or it might better suit your family to journey to a special location—a mountain, the beach, another country, or a theme park. You might also consider journeys that are not as inward focused. Doing a short-term mission trip together as a family can be a profound experience.

Jesus Discipled through Milestones

Jesus participated in many of the religious traditions and milestones of the Jewish faith growing up. He went on pilgrimages with his family to Jerusalem for festivals like the Passover and the Feast of Tabernacles. Jesus attended weddings and the ensuing celebrations. But Jesus not only participated in preexisting ceremonies and traditions; he also clarified and redesigned some of them in order to remind us about him.

We talked earlier in this chapter about how Christ commanded baptism as a milestone ritual of repentance and life in God. Baptism is a ceremony filled with symbolism for Christians of what Christ has done for us in salvation. Similarly, Jesus instituted Communion as a meal to be traditionally practiced by those who follow him. He took the yearly Passover meal and showed how it had always pointed forward toward his sacrifice and how, for Christians, it would point back to his broken body and shed blood for us at the cross. This ritual is a regular reminder of all that we have in Christ and all he has done for us. He said, "'As often as you drink it, [do this] in remembrance of me.' For as often as you eat this bread and drink the cup, you proclaim the Lord's death until he comes" (1 Cor. 11:25–26). Even now, the cross is our most common Christian symbol—one that reminds you, very specifically, of what God did for you.

Examples in Scripture

The Bible has many instances where God's people were given something to remind them of God and his faithfulness. Consider the following passages.

- *The Rainbow* (Gen. 9:12–17). God gave his people a sign for all time to remind them of his wrath and his promise.
- *Building Altars* (Gen. 8:20; 12:7–8; 35:1; Ex. 17:15; Josh. 8:30; Judg. 6:24; 1 Sam. 7:17; 2 Sam. 24:25). God's people built altars in order to honor God, to commemorate what he had accomplished, and to remind the people of what God was like.
- *Festivals and Holy Days* (Ex. 12:1–20, 26–27; 13:14; Lev. 16). God initiated several holy days (holidays) and festivals to remind his people of his goodness, power, and history of faithfulness.
- *The Jar of Manna* (Ex. 16:31–33). God commanded Moses to fill a jar with manna so that future generations would be able to see the keepsake and be reminded of how God cared for his people in the wilderness.
- *The Rescuer* (Ex. 20:2; Deut. 7:18; 26:8). Throughout the Old Testament, God reminded his people time and time again of one of their history's most profound events—how he had rescued them from slavery in Egypt.
- *The Stones of Remembrance* (Josh. 4). God instructed Joshua to place twelve stones (for the twelve tribes of Israel) next to the Jordan River so that the people would be reminded of how God

provided a way into the Promised Land. This also provided a way to tell the next generation about God's provision.

- *Ebenezer* (1 Sam. 7:12). Samuel placed a stone near a battlefield to remind the people that God is their help and wins their battles for them.
- *Jesus Gets His Name* (Matt. 1:20–21). Names, name changes, and even nicknames often have meaning in the Bible. They commemorated some change in a person's life or pointed toward God's mission for an individual.
- *The Last Supper* (1 Cor. 11:23–26). Jesus instituted a ritual meal in which his people would be reminded of his broken body and shed blood on the cross.
- *The People of God Are Called Christians* (Acts 11:25–26). To designate the disciples as those who follow Christ, they were given the title "Christians."
- *Baptizing the Jailer* (Acts 16:25–34). In response to the Lord saving him and adopting him as his son, the jailer was baptized and then cooked a meal to celebrate with his household.

Family Discipleship Milestone Ideas

Birthdays

- Have family members take turns encouraging the birthday child or parent with ways they've seen him or her grow that year, and then pray for the next year.
- Invite friends and neighbors to celebrate what the Lord has done in the life of the child or parent and pray for even more growth.
- Set individual spiritual goals for the next year.

Holidays

- Read Advent scriptures leading up to Christmas.
- Read Lenten scriptures leading up to Easter.
- Bake a birthday cake for Jesus at Christmas.
- Serve together somewhere for a holiday.
- Invite unbelieving friends or neighbors to celebrate a holiday with you.

- Commemorate Thanksgiving by creatively expressing what each of you is grateful for through prayer, crafts, or sharing.
- Celebrate the New Year by making spiritually focused family resolutions or goals.
- On Veteran's Day, write letters to soldiers and pray for those serving in the military.

Anniversaries

- If you're married, celebrate your anniversary with your whole family. Have the kids celebrate and share creatively what God has done in keeping Mom and Dad together.
- Commemorate a loved one who has died on the anniversary of the death, and leverage the opportunity to testify to the faithfulness of God and the reality of our hope with him in eternity.
- Celebrate the anniversary of your child's baptism by treating it like you would a birthday—with a cake, cards, blessings, and presents.

Family Adventures

- A family mission trip
- A family camping trip/retreat
- Annual family vacations
- Moving to a new house or city, getting a new job
- A family road trip

Rites of Passage

- Baby dedication
- A ceremony with close friends or family to acknowledge a transition to manhood or womanhood
- Graduation
- Winning or completing a competition

Ideas by Stages

At Birth

- Choose a name for your child that has a spiritual meaning.

- Use a baby dedication resource to dedicate your child to the Lord along with your faith family.
- Choose a verse to pray over your child nightly as you put him or her to bed, and share that verse with your community.

One Year Old

- Throw a birthday party with your family, close friends, and neighbors. Testify to the goodness of God that you've seen in your child's life, reaffirm your commitment to raising your child in the way of the Lord, and invite some friends to pray for specific things you'd like to see in your child's life.

Two to Four Years Old

- Get your child his or her first Bible. There are many good options for children with pictures, summaries, and discussion questions.

Five to Ten Years Old

- Take your child on annual family adventures where you explore, serve, and talk about God.
- Involve your children in annual birthday and holiday celebrations to bless them and cultivate a love and fear of God.

Eleven to Fourteen Years Old

- Have a more substantial talk about purity and sexuality.
- Give your children their first study Bible.
- Find an opportunity for them to serve regularly in the church.
- Add significant responsibilities.
- Hope and pray to celebrate their salvation in baptism if it hasn't already happened.
- Consider having them join the family in taking Communion.
- Send them or go with them on their first mission trip.

Fifteen to Seventeen Years Old

- Organize a rite-of-passage ceremony or adventure.
- Celebrate earning a driver's license.

- Add responsibilities that build the independence your child will need after high school.

Eighteen Years and Older
- Celebrate a graduation, college acceptance, job placement, launch into independence, and so on.

Conclusion

Family discipleship milestones are marking and making occasions to celebrate and commemorate significant spiritual milestones of God's work in the life of the family and individual child. Milestones can be momentous events, so they may require a greater level of creativity and effort, but that is not required. Spiritual milestones can simply be new ways to take advantage of existing celebrations in your family's life. However your plan works out, celebrating noteworthy moments in a way that is more memorable can correspondingly have a greater impact on your family's life. Milestones are a tremendous opportunity to enjoy and share in commemorating all that the Lord has done!

Questions

1. If you could relive one day of your life over and over again, which would you choose?

2. If you could make it so that one day of your life never happened, which would you choose?

3. What are the most profoundly joyful and wonderful things that you have ever done or that have ever happened to you? How have you seen God work through them?

4. What are the most profoundly sorrowful and distressful things that you have ever done or that have ever happened to you? How have you seen God work through them?

5. Are there events in your past that you wish had been marked more profoundly or intentionally with gospel truth? What are they?

6. You can see in many of the scriptural examples that milestones often include a physical reminder. Can you think of some items, rituals, or places that serve as reminders to you of God's faithfulness in your life?

7. Did you have any family traditions growing up that you'd love to see continue in your family? Do you have any family traditions now that could be better leveraged for a Christian purpose?

8. What family traditions could you create in the way you celebrate birthdays that will bless each of your children as individuals and point them to love and fear the Lord?

9. What are some common rites of passage for boys and girls in our society? What are some common or unique rites of passage you might consider for your own child?

10. A pilgrimage is a trip with spiritual significance. Is there anywhere that your family could travel as a kind of family pilgrimage?

Making a Milestone Plan

Spend some time considering the different life stages and events that your child might encounter and design some family discipleship milestones that you could dedicate to the Lord along the way. Look back on the list of ideas in this chapter as you try to formulate your plan using figure 3: Milestone Plan.

Example Milestone Plan

AGE	SAMPLE	IDEAS / PLANS
BIRTH	· Baby dedication with Home Group; choose life verse for child	
1	· Birthday party with Community	
2-4	· Gift of their first Bible	
5-10	· Annual family vacations	
11-14	· First communion; start serving at church	
15-17	· Organize "rite of passage"	
18 & UP	· Graduation party	

Fig. 3

Milestone Plan

	YOUR IDEAS
IDEAS FOR FAMILY TRADITIONS	
IDEAS FOR FAMILY ADVENTURES	
IDEAS FOR GIFTS/MEMENTOS TO BESTOW	
IDEAS FOR BIRTHDAY/ ANNIVERSARY TRADITIONS	

"Tell your children of it, / and let your children tell their children, / and their children to another generation." —Joel 1:3

You are as much serving God in looking after your own children and training them up in God's fear, and minding the house, and making your household a church for God, as you would be if you had been called to lead an army to battle for the Lord of hosts![1] —Charles Spurgeon

"Most assuredly God will require an account of the children from your hands, for they are His, and only lent to your care and keeping. The task assigned you is no easy one, especially in these superlatively evil days. Nevertheless, if trustfully and earnestly sought, the grace of God will be found sufficient in this responsibility as in others. The Scriptures supply us with rules to go by, with promises to lay hold of, and, we may add, with fearful warnings lest we treat the matter lightly."[2] —Arthur W. Pink

"It is easier to build strong children than to repair broken men."[3] —Frederick Douglass

"God knows the feelings of discouragement, inadequacy, and failure which conscientious parents feel. But it was His idea to make them parents and to give them this particular set of children. He knew they would not do a perfect job. He is Father to the parents, and promises every kind of help they need. He stands beside them in every situation, ready to give wisdom as needed and grace to help in time of need if only they will turn to Him and ask for it."[4] —Elisabeth Elliot

"The authority with which God has invested you, as parents and governors of families, is a talent committed to your trust and which you are bound to improve to your Master's honor."[5] —George Whitefield

"To you the message is simple—fly at once, with your household, to the throne of grace! Cease to consider it as a matter of indifference, or an affair of variable custom. The neglect is most serious. It is your loss, and the loss of your offspring. It is your sin. It calls for repentance, and for reformation, which is the criterion of repentance . . . you should begin now."[6] —J. W. Alexander

Conclusion

Parting Encouragement

When it comes to family discipleship, low-hanging fruit is everywhere. You do not need to create amazing productions or have an archive of profound insights at the ready. Family discipleship does not have to be intricate or complicated. You just need a willingness to focus on the child who is in front of you, and together focus on the God who is everywhere. Even if your kids are practically grown and you are just getting started, be encouraged that all is not lost. One of the most powerful moments you can have with your kids is to own the fact that you wish you would have done these things in the past, that you love them, and that you want to start working through this framework together.

You are a parent walking in a relationship with Christ, the King of kings, who "is able to make all grace abound to you, so that having all sufficiency in all things at all times, you may abound in every good work" (2 Cor. 9:8). So you can be Christlike in how you address your household. You can have a relentlessly gracious heart, a gentle touch, a glad tongue, and a granite resolve. At some point, and perhaps often, you will surely encounter disinterest and resistance, which you will readily answer with peaceful persistence. Parents, do not surrender to opposition. "Be strong and courageous. Do not be frightened, and do not be dismayed, for the LORD your God is with you wherever you go" (Josh. 1:9).

Christ is the master of your heart, and he himself came not to be served but to serve and give his life away for others (Matt. 20:28). You can likewise tirelessly serve the needs of your children by being strong when they need strength and being wise when they need wisdom. You can always be prepared to make a defense to your children anytime they ask you for a reason for the hope that is in you, and yet you'll always do it with gentleness and respect (1 Pet. 3:15).

You can have the confidence and competence to boldly dare to lead, risking failures. Mistakes will be made but risks must be taken in order to boldly endeavor to fulfill your role. In the Chandler home, we have failed a million times, and I'm positive our kids will forget most of those. Errors can be undone. As a wrong turn can be compensated for by recalculating your route, you will walk back your missteps and then proceed down the right path undeterred. Errors can be overcome. A heartfelt apology and a hug can reunite a wounded friendship; own your mistakes and liberally apply grace to one another. Errors go hand in hand with human efforts. But don't only *accept* that mistakes will be made, *embrace* that every one is an opportunity for grace and growth. Persevere undaunted and grateful for the lessons.

It is great to parent carefully, but we should remain mindful not to wander into cowardice. You have been entrusted with the rearing of the next generation, and that responsibility must be handled thoughtfully and wisely. You should be careful when discerning what influences you allow, which situations your kids should face, and which they should flee from. Being careful, though, should not make you a coward, sheltering your kids from any chance of failure or discomfort. We hope you never have to see your children face immense spiritual, physical, or emotional danger, but if or when they do, we pray you will not react in a spirit of timidity. We pray you will react bravely, trusting in the Lord.

We also pray you would not be careless or reckless with their lives, disregarding wisdom to thrust them into the fray. Parent courageously, but do not stray into carelessness. Balance trust in God with godly wisdom to avoid both overprotecting and overexposing your kids. There are a great many dangers to be faced in this world, and you must have the backbone to help your children face them with both tenacity and wisdom. Strive to trade self-centered fears and worries for God-centered trust and wisdom. Let courage and carefulness direct your steps as you labor to raise kids who will walk in the fear of the Lord.

As you've worked through the framework for family discipleship in this book, we pray that it has been useful to you. We hope that you've been blessed by the conversations you've had with your family and close community. These lists, ideas, thoughts to process, and questions are intended to encourage and equip you in your strategy, but don't get too attached to the details of your plans. Sometimes following the unexpected detour is the most exciting and fruitful part of the adventure you've been called to. The methods and means presented are meant to whet your appetite for the word of God and for the pursuit of spiritual health in your home. Feed that hunger. Foster a culture of development and dedication in your household. Ask yourself, "What do I want my kids to be able to do on their own?" and take steps to train them to do it. Now you know the importance of family discipleship, but don't be surprised by how easy it will be to forget and become distracted. Sometimes it is easy to wake up, but it is hard to stay awake. You will get tired, and you will be tempted to relent or let things slide because you are exhausted by everything else life throws at you, "but they who wait for the LORD shall renew their strength" (Isa. 40:31).

Don't be surprised if radical changes in your family do not happen overnight. Personal heart change and sanctification, in you as well as your children, can be remarkably slow. Many of the transformations the Lord works in this world are imperceptibly incremental, progressing degree by undetectable degree. Only a fool plants an acorn in the evening and comes back in the morning looking for an oak. Your work to cultivate that change will be painstaking and gradual, unfolding over a lifetime.

If family discipleship rhythms will be a major shift for your household, it all might feel like too much too quickly. But you also don't want to do too little too slowly. Wisely navigate the pace of introducing a new sustainable rhythm that weaves gospel conversations into your family interactions in sincere ways. God is the world's foremost expert on you and your family. He has left you with a lot to teach them, but you don't have to teach everything in one night. Regardless of the size of the meal, you can consume it just one bite at a time; eat any quicker and you'll choke. But eat too slowly or rarely, and you may starve. Don't let the progress of your instruction drift to nonexistence in the name of pacing yourself.

We are eager to see how God uses the framework to lead your family into an ever-deepening relationship with him. Think about all that you've just walked through and consider your plan. How will you pursue your own spiritual health in ways that bless your family? How will you gather your family at appointed times for studying and practicing the word of God together? How will you take advantage of impromptu moments throughout the day to talk about what God is like as well as being like God? How will you commemorate the big moments in your family's spiritual life?

As you start to work out these ideas in your own home, know that we are praying for you and we hope you'll lean on your church to help you and walk beside you. We encourage you to be diligent to seek accountability for how you want to lead your home as well as to hold others accountable. Be an expert in follow-up and follow-through. Love one another as God, in Christ, has loved you, and rejoice in doing so. Being a parent is a privilege and a joy. Yes, parenting is not always easy, but it's just as true that it's not always hard. Yes, you will make mistakes, but it's also true that sometimes you will nail it!

Let it never be said of you that you gave up on family discipleship before you gave everything you had, leaning on the sufficient grace of God. Do not forsake your sacred duty. Our prayer is that one day you will be able to look each of your children in the eye and sincerely say, "As for you, continue in what you have learned and have firmly believed, knowing from whom you learned it and how from childhood you have been acquainted with the sacred writings, which are able to make you wise for salvation through faith in Christ Jesus" (2 Tim. 3:14–15).

Appendix

A Word to Church and School Leaders

"I know not how a minister can employ his time, studies, and pen better (next to the conviction and conversion of particular souls), than impressing upon householders a care of the souls under their charge."[1] —Oliver Heywood

"Many Christians today are praying for revival in the church, but there will never be revival in the church unless there is revival in the home."[2] —Howard Hendricks

We believe that the more home-centered your ministry focus becomes, the more success you will see in leading every generation to follow Christ. The home that practices sincere Christian discipleship is your greatest ally.

Unfortunately, many of the discipleship muscles of the body of Christ have atrophied. We wrote this book because we want the exercises in this book to push the families in your congregation or school into healthy discipleship. Making disciples is a primary call for any believer, and yet it's often absent from the lives of those in our local congregations, including inside their homes. As a leader in the Christian community, you have the opportunity to challenge, resource, and encourage those under your care to take up the mantle of family discipleship as the Lord has commanded.

As we wrote this book, we kept you in mind in addition to parents in general. We hope this book is one you can put into the hands of the parents at your school and the families in your congregation in order to greatly bless your Christian community. When those you lead are fully engaged in family discipleship, they will benefit, and so will you.

In addition, your leaders must be the ones to exemplify family discipleship. You know that elders, as the examples to follow in your churches, not only *ought* to lead their homes in family discipleship, but they *must* do it. For a man to be an elder he absolutely has to "manage his own household well, with all dignity keeping his children submissive, for if someone does not know how to manage his own household, how will he care for God's church?" (1 Tim. 3:4–5). Even if a man is the most gifted organizational leader a church has, if he is not a good disciple-maker at home, he is disqualified from consideration as an overseer.

The framework of *time, moments*, and *milestones* makes a great tool for evaluation, accountability, and training when it comes to the readiness of those who have the privilege of leadership. Whether it's asking an elder candidate what *time, moments*, and *milestones* look like for his family or asking staff members if there have been any encouraging examples of the Lord's work through the framework in their homes lately, the shared language from this book helps foster a culture where family discipleship is important and normal as well as celebrated.

Though we are partial, we believe that the content of this resource is exactly what we would want the families of our schools and the members of our congregations studying and implementing in their own homes. Make it a gift to a family in your community when they have a child or when they enroll a child in your school. Make it a resource for your teachers or family ministry staff to help them clarify the expectations of parents. However you see fit, we hope the work we have put into this material will bless your community in profound ways to serve the God we follow together, for the glory of the one true God, for the sake of the coming kingdom, and for the salvation of the next generation.

I rejoiced greatly to find some of
your children walking in the truth,
just as we were commanded
by the Father.
2 John 4

Notes

Introduction

1. Charles H. Spurgeon, ed., "The Kind of Revival Wanted by the Church," in *The Sword and the Trowel: A Record of Combat with Sin and of Labour for the Lord* (London: Passmore & Alabaster, 1887), 515–16.

2. Billy Graham, "Why Didn't Someone Tell Me How Hard It Is Being a Parent?," Billy Graham Evangelistic Association, February 20, 2006, https://billygraham .org/answer/why-didnt-someone-tell-me-how-hard-it-is-being-a-parent/.

3. Elisabeth Elliot, *A Lamp for My Feet* (Ann Arbor, MI: Vine Books, 1985), 137.

4. Martin Luther, *Christian Life in the World*, vol. 5 of *The Annotated Luther*, eds. Hans J. Hillerbrand, Kirsi I. Stjerna, and Timothy J. Wengert (Minneapolis: Fortress Press, 2017), 75.

Chapter 1: The Family That Disciples

1. Charles H. Spurgeon, *Spurgeon's Sermons on Family and Home* (Grand Rapids, MI: Kreger, 1995), 92.

2. Tony Evans, *Raising Kingdom Kids: Giving Your Child a Living Faith* (Carol Stream, IL: Tyndale, 2014), 33.

3. Jonathan Edwards, "Farewell Sermon," in *The Sermons of Jonathan Edwards: A Reader*, ed. Wilson H. Kimnach, Kenneth P. Minkema, and Douglas A. Sweeney (New Haven, CT: Yale University Press, 1999), 236.

4. Howard G. Hendricks, *God's Blueprint for Family Living* (Lincoln, NE: The Good News Broadcasting Association, 1973), back cover.

Chapter 2: The Foundation

1. C. H. Spurgeon, *Come, Ye Children: A Book for Parents and Teachers on the Christian Training of Children* (Pasadena, TX: Pilgrim Publications, 1975), chap. 8.

2. Martin Luther King Jr., "The Negro Family: A Challenge to National Action," address delivered at the University of Chicago, Chicago, IL, January 27, 1966.

3. John Calvin, *Sermons on Genesis, Chapters 11:5–20:7: Forty-Eight Sermons Delivered in Geneva between 24 January 1560 and 15 May 1560*, ed. Rob Roy McGregor (Edinburgh: Banner of Truth, 2012), 671.

4. James Waddel Alexander, *Thoughts on Family Worship* (1847; repr., Tomball, TX: Legacy Ministry Publications, 2010), 124.

5. George Grant, *The Courage and Character of Theodore Roosevelt: A Hero among Leaders* (Nashville: Cumberland House, 2005), 167.

6. Nancy Guthrie, *The One Year Praying through the Bible for Your Kids* (Carol Stream, IL: Tyndale Momentum, 2016), xi.

Chapter 3: Modeling

1. As quoted in Timothy Z. Witmer, *The Shepherd Leader at Home: Knowing, Leading, Protecting, and Providing for Your Family* (Wheaton, IL: Crossway, 2012), 87.
2. Elisabeth Elliot, *The Shaping of a Christian Family: How My Parents Nurtured My Faith* (Grand Rapids, MI: Revell, 2005), 99.
3. Thomas Watson, *The Ten Commandments* (1692; repr., Edinburgh: Banner of Truth, rev. ed., 1965), 137.
4. Arthur W. Pink, *Ten Commandments* (Sovereign Grace Publishers, 2007), 64.
5. Beth Moore, "Parenting Pointers with Beth Moore," CBN.com, September 17, 2013, https://www1.cbn.com/700club/parenting-pointers-beth-moore-0.
6. Howard G. Hendricks, *God's Blueprint for Family Living* (Lincoln, NE: The Good News Broadcasting Association, 1973), 54.
7. Theodore Roosevelt, *Theodore Roosevelt on Bravery: Lessons from the Most Courageous Leader of the Twentieth Century* (New York: Skyhorse Publishing, 2015), np.

Chapter 4: Time

1. C. H. Spurgeon, "A Promise for Us and for Our Children," in *Spurgeon's Sermons*, vol. 10 (Grand Rapids, MI: Baker, 1987), 134.
2. James Waddel Alexander, *Thoughts on Family Worship* (1847; repr., Tomball, TX: Legacy Ministry Publications, 2010), 39.
3. Howard G. Hendricks, *God's Blueprint for Family Living* (Lincoln, NE: The Good News Broadcasting Association, 1973), 59.
4. Sally Lloyd-Jones, "When You've Got to Figure Out How to Get You and Your Family through Storms," Ann Voskamp website, June 11, 2015, https://annvoskamp.com/2015/06/when-youve-got-to-figure-out-how-to-get-you-and-your-family-through-storms/.
5. John Bunyan, *Christian Behaviour: Being the Fruits of True Christianity: Teaching Husbands, Wives, Parents, Children, Masters, Servants, etc., How to Walk so as to Please God. With a Word of Direction to All Back-Sliders* (London, 1674), np.

Chapter 5: Moments

1. C. H. Spurgeon, *Come, Ye Children: A Book for Parents and Teachers on the Christian Training of Children* (Pasadena, TX: Pilgrim Publications, 1975), chap. 2.
2. Richard Baxter, *The Poor Man's Family Book* (Boston: Joseph Noble, LowGate, and John Noble, 1818), 105.
3. Elisabeth Elliot, *The Shaping of a Christian Family: How My Parents Nurtured My Faith* (Grand Rapids, MI: Revell, 2005), 120.
4. Matthew Henry, *A Church in the House* (sermon preached 1704; repr., Shawnee, KS: Gideon House Books, 2015), 5.
5. Ann Voskamp, "10 Point Manifesto for Joyful Parenting," Ann Voskamp website, 2010, https://annvoskamp.com/10-points-of-joyful-parenting-printable/.
6. Marilynne Robinson, *Gilead* (New York: Picador, 2004), 248.

Chapter 6: Milestones
1. Charles H. Spurgeon, *Evening by Evening or Readings by Eventide for the Family or the Closet* (New York: Sheldon and Company, 1869), 194.
2. St. Augustine of Hippo, *The Confessions of Saint Augustine* (London: J. M. Dent & Sons Ltd., 1939), 48.
3. Francis Fisher Browne, *The Every-Day Life of Abraham Lincoln* (London, 1914), 239.
4. Billy Graham, *Nearing Home: Thoughts on Life, Faith and Finishing Well* (Nashville: Thomas Nelson, 2011), 119.

Conclusion: Parting Encouragement
1. Charles H. Spurgeon, "The Weaned Child," in *The Complete Works of C. H. Spurgeon*, vol. 21, *Sermons 1210–1270* (Harrington, DE: Delmarva Publications, 2013), Kindle.
2. Arthur W. Pink, *Ten Commandments* (Sovereign Grace Publishers, 2007), 62–63.
3. As quoted in Korie Robertson, Willie Robertson, and Chrys Howard, *Strong and Kind: Raising Kids of Character* (Nashville: W Publishing Group, 2017), 201.
4. Elisabeth Elliot, *The Shaping of a Christian Family: How My Parents Nurtured My Faith* (Grand Rapids, MI: Revell, 2005), 146.
5. John Gillies, *Memoirs of George Whitefield* (New Ipswich, NH: Pietan Publications, 1993), 450.
6. James Waddel Alexander, *Thoughts on Family Worship* (1847; repr., Tomball, TX: Legacy Ministry Publications, 2010), 173.

Appendix: A Word to Church and School Leaders
1. Oliver Heywood, *A Family Altar Erected to the Honour of the Eternal God or, A Solemn Essay to Promote the Worship of God in Private Houses* (London: T. Parkhurst, 1693), np.
2. Howard G. Hendricks, *God's Blueprint for Family Living* (Lincoln, NE: Good News Broadcasting Association, 1973), 68.

Scripture Index